THE

TENTH

CIRCLE

OF HELL

THE

TENTH

CIRCLE

OF HELL

A Memoir of Life in the

Death Camps of Bosnia

REZAK HUKANOVIĆ

Translated from the Bosnian by Colleen London and Midhat Ridjanović

Edited from the original by Ammiel Alcalay

A New Republic Book
BasicBooks
A Division of HarperCollins*Publishers*

The publisher gratefully acknowledges the help of Ammiel Alcalay, Dr. David Benjamin, and Svein Monnesland in the publication of this book.

Chapters 1 and 2 of this work have previously appeared in *The New Republic*.

Published by BasicBooks,
A Division of HarperCollins Publishers, Inc.

Designed by Elliott Beard

FIRST EDITION

Library of Congress Cataloging-in-Publication Data
Hukanović, Rezak
    The tenth circle of hell : a memoir of life in the death camps of Bosnia / by Rezak Hukanović ; translated by Colleen London and Midhat Ridjanović; edited from the original by Ammiel Alcalay. — 1st ed.
        p.   cm.
    ISBN 0-465-08408-7
    1. Concentration camps—Bosnia and Herzegovina. 2. Yugoslav War, 1991–   —Personal narratives, Bosnian. I. Title.
    DR1313.7.P74H85 1996
    949.702'4—dc20   96-16631
                                          CIP

96 97 98 99 00 ❖/HC 10 9 8 7 6 5 4 3 2 1

Foreword

ELIE WIESEL

Dante was wrong. Hell consists not of nine circles, but of ten. Rezak Hukanović takes you to the latest one, the most dreadful and the most heartbreaking. And we know where to find it. Hell, according to Rabbi Nahman of Bratzlav, the great Hasidic storyteller and thinker, is not in the world to come but in this one. We have only to look at Bosnia-Herzegovina during the period of its occupation by the Serbs to see that this is so. We have only to read this poignant and overwhelming, often unbearable, account, by a man who has witnessed and lived in the flesh the tragedy of the oppressed and the persecuted of the former Yugoslavia.

Hukanović recounts a story of hatred, cruelty, and murder. I do not know why he writes in the third person, for it is evident that this is a personal testimony. It will keep you from sleeping.

Let us acknowledge right away that this tragedy could have been averted. If only the German Chancellor Helmut Kohl had not so swiftly—too swiftly—recognized Croatia's independence; if only the Western allies had resisted his pressure and refused to follow suit; if only our country and our government had found the wisdom and the courage to intervene immediately—how many human lives could have been saved?

But the great powers preferred to keep their distance. They did not understand that a nation is not great in its armed might but in its capacity and its will to act in the name of those ethical principles without which a society cannot be considered civilized. It is better not to mention the United Nations. Charged with the protection of the weak, this organization demonstrates its own weakness, its lack of initiative, as soon as it is called upon to oppose aggressors of any kind.

It is false to pretend that we did not know what was happening on the ground. We knew. The media conscientiously fulfilled its duty to inform. We were aware of the horrors that were unfolding there. The rapes, the tortures, the humiliations at Prijedor. Certainly it was wrong, in the beginning, to exaggerate by comparing these crimes to the atrocities committed by the Germans during the Holocaust. Omarska was not Auschwitz. Nothing, anywhere, can be compared to Auschwitz. But what took place at Omarska was sufficiently serious to shake the world's conscience and to justify international intervention and international solidarity.

It is imperative, therefore, to read this book, and to ensure that it is read. One emerges from it as from a terrible nightmare, crushed by a hatred at once ancestral and constantly present, weighty. Here are men who know each other well, neighbors who greet each other in the street, friends of many years standing who, suddenly, poisoned by patriotic and ethnic fanaticism, become fierce and bitter enemies.

How to explain such cruelty, such sadism, among people who only yesterday lived in brotherhood with their victims of today?

Why, among them, such a thirst to hurt, to injure, to humiliate human beings whose only wrong—whose only "crime"—is to believe in Mohammed rather than in Jesus?

There are, in this narrative, scenes of terror that speak of madness. Thirst, hunger, gang rapes, exhaustion, filth, blows, insults; skulls shattered, sexual organs torn out, stomachs ripped open: the soldier assassins of Radovan Karadžić, their expressions gleeful and sneering, stop at nothing to dehumanize their prisoners. There are the torturers who order an old man to make love to a young woman in public. And the father forced to witness the torture of his son. And the son who sees his father bludgeoned to death in front of him. And there are those who "never came back"—a terrifying phrase which recurs frequently throughout these pages.

At the same time, here and there, we encounter touching moments. Prisoners who help each other, who nurse the tortured and force themselves to console those near death. We learn, even, of a Serb soldier who retains his humanity: in secret, he gives bread and soup to an old friend. It is thus: in hell, all things can be found.

The author writes also about Manjača, the camp in Banja Luka. I visited it myself. I met the commander, Lieutenant Colonel Božidar Popović. I was able to speak with miserable prisoners who, in the darkness, murmured words I could not understand. That is to say: I feel close to this story, I tried to bear witness for its victims.

In the end, they were freed. Their principal executioners have been charged with crimes against humanity. And as I write these lines, hope seems to quicken. Fortunately, the Dayton accords continue to hold.

And yet I cannot forget the man who, upon leaving the prison and the camp, cried out, "Lord, may you never forgive them."

Translated by Claire Messud

Although written in the third person, *The Tenth Circle of Hell* is a firsthand account of life in a Serb concentration camp. The author, Rezak Hukanović, was seized on May 30, 1992, in his hometown of Prijedor, a small northwestern Bosnian city of 112,000. The course of aggression against non-Serbs in Prijedor was typical of the war in Bosnia-Herzegovina: the occupying Serb nationalist forces systematically seized and, in many cases, murdered the local elites—mayors, doctors, lawyers, judges, teachers, engineers, and cultural figures. (A journalist's account of the ethnic cleansing of Prijedor can be found in Roy Guttman's *A Witness to Genocide*, which records many of the same names as victims, as well as similar details of the operations in the camps.)

Rezak Hukanović is one of the cultural figures from Prijedor who managed to survive. In coming to write of his experiences in the Omarska and Manjača camps, Hukanović felt that using the third person would be the most effective means of conveying the mixture of the macabre and the mundane that constituted the lives of Bosnian prisoners. He has also explained that he chose to use a third-person narrator because he felt, at the time, that the brutal events he endured—as well as the complicit behavior of former friends and neighbors he witnessed—must have been happening to someone else.

Chapter One

Saturday, May 30, 1992. A sunny day. Djemo didn't wake up until around 9:30. Actually, it was the deafening sound of shooting outside that woke him up. For the past few days, since the shooting started in Prijedor, Djemo hadn't slept at his place. It wasn't safe. One side of his house faced the main road, while the other, the side that went against the light, looked down on a dense acacia grove. Even though it was almost in the center of town, the grove seemed like a thick forest.

Only last night shots had been fired from around Pećani, on the other side of the grove, more frequently and with more force than usual. It had taken Djemo a long time to fall asleep. He still remembered the shooting on New Year's Eve. Bursts of fire from all kinds of weapons had rung out from Pećani until daybreak. They had seemed to be competing to see who could fire the longest round. Incendiary bullets had pierced the sky above Prijedor.

It hadn't seemed like a good omen.

One morning Djemo had found a bullet hole in his bedroom window, the one overlooking the acacia grove. The bullet had gone through the closed shutters on the outside of the house and through the double panes of glass to pierce the wall over the bed a few inches from the big mirror. Djemo knew that no one would have shot at his house deliberately. He hadn't given anyone reason to hold a grudge, and he wasn't particularly interested in politics, especially not what passed for it these days. All that tactical maneuvering between Serbs and Muslims (there were very few Croats in the area) struck him as ridiculous.

The guys he knew split up into Muslims and Serbs

only when they played soccer on the banks of the Sana River on hot summer days. Games like that were always organized by Eko, the local cutup who crooned in the bars of Prijedor. Sometimes the Serbs would win, sometimes the Muslims, but it would always end with beer and a barbecue, masterfully laid out by Eko himself. The drinks and the food, of course, were on the losing team. Over drinks they would sing together, softly, just for the hell of it.

But those were different times. Now the Serbs had taken control of Prijedor overnight, and they were carrying out their usual theatrics. Walking around in army uniforms, they had barricaded all the roads leading into town, a practice that had come to be called "the log revolution." One morning Serb flags appeared on the town hall, the police station, and the Prijedor Hotel. In its long, rich history, Prijedor had never experienced a stranger occupation.

Its inhabitants, in panic, kept still. Someone emptied his rounds into the calm.

The occupation of Prijedor had taken place over a month ago. All the Muslims—along with the few Croats who lived in the city—had been dismissed from their jobs. The schools were closed. The Serbs took control of all the radio and television transmitters and began broadcasting their own programs. The newspapers, except for the Serbian ones, stopped appearing or, at any rate, could no longer be found in town. A media blockade.

"A power struggle," Djemo said to himself. "I'll be fine if things stay like this." Life had been good to him until then: a house, a car, a decent salary, a wife and two sons, one sixteen, the other just turned twelve. Actually, he hadn't been getting along too well with his wife. Djemo burned the candle at both ends a little more than he should have for someone his age, especially since he had a family. He could be seen in bars with a drink in his hand, hanging out with a younger crowd. And with girls too. That was something his wife Alma wasn't the least bit crazy about. But she figured he'd settle down, because of the kids.

He hadn't gone out lately. Since last Saturday, when the army had been shooting at Hambarine, a village about ten miles from Prijedor, he hadn't gone anywhere. He spent his time just watching movies on TV or playing cards with neighbors and family. "Neighbors and relatives never visit each other this much," he thought. That night he had played cards very late at his cousin Fadil's place and ended up staying over, along with the rest of the family.

Fadil's house was right across the street from his own, so he could at least see if anything strange was going on at home. And that morning, something strange did happen.

His cousin Fadil knocked on the door of the room where they were sleeping to tell them the news. The local radio station announced that Prijedor had—as the announcers put it—been attacked by "Muslim extremists." This item was repeated a number of times. And then, every ten minutes, they heard the following message: "Citizens are requested to remain in their homes and apartments for the sake of their own security."

It was sunny, a real spring day, but no good was to come of it. There was tension in the air; a curious apprehension hovered over the city.

With the constant brainwashing the media was subjecting everyone to, it didn't take much for someone to cross the line and act in ways they might never have imagined. People still kept telling each other nothing ugly would happen around here, but they didn't really believe it. Over in Sarajevo, they knew, a real war was being waged. "That's a long way off," they used to say. "These are the Kozara Mountains; people have been living together here for ages."

But then the streets were full of strangers, armed to the teeth, with all kinds of insignias on their uniforms. And everyone knew that only the Serbs were armed— down to the last man, including the children. Camouflage fatigues, an automatic rifle with at least two rounds draped across each shoulder, a knife in a leather sheath, a few grenades: this was the identity card that established Serb loyalty. Only an armed Serb was a real Serb. All the other Serbs were against them, against their "Serb Republic," which they had already proclaimed, although they themselves knew it was just a pipe dream: a state within the internationally recognized state of Bosnia-Herzegovina.

The new authority enforced measures that brought all non-Serbs into a state of submission and passivity, while its new cadres carried out orders with genuine gusto, distorting normal ties between people beyond the point of absurdity. They embarked on a systematic instigation of hatred toward anyone who could possibly be thought of, or felt to be, non-Serb. Indiscriminate moral perversion became routine among Serbs. It was astonishing to witness the chameleonlike transformation of former friends and acquaintances as they turned into crazed servants of the new authority. To these Serbs, Bosnia-Herzegovina was a "former republic." This became a fixed term in the Serb media, on TV Banja Luka and TV Pale, that factory of lies, as well as in the *Banja Luka Daily Voice* (which later changed its name to the *Serb Voice*).

Djemo knew very well that, in a war like this, truth had to be killed first.

The local paper in Prijedor, the *Kozara Herald*, became no less Serb than the rest of the media. Every Friday the newsstands sold fresh lies. The *Herald* editor and now the sole boss of the paper, Mile Mutić, along with Živko Ećim and Rade Mutić, his brothers in religious and ideological arms, produced lies in three shifts; even worse, these local scribblers hijacked the once-respected term "journalism." Mutić, an unscrupulous reporter who had never even pretended to be a decent guy, a reserve officer in the former Yugoslav People's

Army, and God knows what else, broadcast threats to the non-Serb population, calling on them to surrender their weapons, even if they had been acquired legally. No one but Serbs could bear arms. This became his battle cry.

The man, if one could call him that, even had the nerve to write poetry, though there was nothing even remotely poetic about him. He seemed to derive particular pleasure from the suffering of others, from dishonoring and humiliating them. Mutić had to be considered one of the founding fathers of the deformation of the history of this city and its people, the people of the Kozara Mountains. The only new history he could envision for his people was the slaughter of other peoples, their total annihilation, a "poetic" fantasy he transformed into a most absurd reality. In this, of course, he had the complete support of the Serb authorities. Morality, journalistic ethics—these were terms he didn't seem to know the meaning of.

Djemo had never found much to like about Mutić during his stints on the local radio station and at the paper. He'd often seen the huge bearded creature around, the obligatory pipe in his mouth and a leather bag slung over his shoulder. This morning Djemo recognized his hoarse voice on the radio. For the ump-teenth time that day Mutić was informing listeners that Prijedor had been "attacked by Muslim extremists." He called on citizens not to leave their homes and guaranteed, on behalf of the "Emergency Committee," their safety and security. He added that all loyal citizens should put a white flag out where it could easily be seen. Even little kids knew what a white flag meant.

Djemo drank his usual morning coffee. He lit a cigarette and took a few drags. From time to time he glanced through the window in the direction of his house. He didn't notice anything unusual. Through another window he looked at the building next to his, about forty yards away, and saw two soldiers armed with rifles on the roof of the building. Every now and then they fired in the direction of Skela, a neighboring residential area. "They can't be trusted," said Djemo, as he moved the table where they were sitting away from the window. Alma had gone over to their place to make breakfast. Soon she came back and put the food on the table. Fadil's wife busied herself around the stove for a while, and then they all sat down for breakfast. The city still thundered with the clatter of automatic weapons.

At some point Fadil looked toward Djemo's place and said, "There are some soldiers around your house." Djemo drew the curtain a little and saw two armed men with face masks cautiously approaching the main entrance of the building, crouching down, with their fingers on the trigger. Just then there was a heavy thump on Fadil's door. It opened, and Djemo turned to see another soldier exactly like the ones he had just seen across the road. He stood by the door with his rifle aimed right at them. "Got any weapons?" he demanded. They were petrified.

"You deaf or what?" By now he was shouting. "Got any weapons or not?"

"No, brother," Fadil was the first to speak. "We don't."

"I'm not your brother, we can't be brothers, *ever!* Got that? How about you?" He signaled to Djemo with his chin.

"I don't have any. I never have!" said Djemo.

With a look of utter disbelief, the soldier walked around the room, without lowering his rifle for even a second; he kept it aimed at the table and everyone sitting around it. "You've got to get out of here," he said, as if they were under his command. "There's shooting all over the place. We'll take you someplace safer until it stops." Brandishing his rifle, he motioned Djemo and Fadil to go out. Fadil got up first and, with his arms raised over his head, moved toward the door. The soldier stepped and, still with the end of his rifle aimed at them, followed Fadil. The children were crying. Then Djemo got up. He put his hands behind his head and, in slow motion (he knew what a quick move might mean in such a situation), walked toward the door.

When he got close to the soldier, he paused a second to steal a glance at him. No, he didn't know him. "Don't be scared, Djemo," the soldier told him. "Nothing's going to happen to you," and it seemed to Djemo that the soldier even tapped him on the shoulder to make his words sound more convincing. Djemo looked hard but couldn't recognize a face behind the dark mask. The man's voice didn't sound familiar either.

He took a few more steps and found himself in the courtyard. There was another soldier there, in a darker uniform, who ordered Djemo and Fadil to keep on going toward the first entrance of the building, next to the acacia grove. Those hundred or so yards lasted forever. Fadil was in front followed by Djemo, who felt the heavy load of a gun barrel on his back, like a burden he was carrying. The air smelled of gunpowder, of things burning. Farther away he could see billowing clouds of black smoke. The Old City was in flames. Djemo wanted to turn toward his house just once more to see what had become of his family, but he didn't dare. He was afraid it might be the last look of his life.

When they came close to the entrance of the building, the soldier behind them left and another one, standing by the entrance, told them to go into the building. They stumbled down a few steps into the cellar, where they could see several neighbors, all Muslims. Around the entrance itself some of their Serb neighbors were milling around with rifles slung over their shoulders. Pero, who lived in the building and knew everyone, said, "You're safer down here. Don't worry. You'll just stay here until all this blows over." Then he even offered everyone some home-brewed plum brandy. They all considered Pero a good neighbor and trusted him, even though no one had much choice in the matter at that point. The bottle went from mouth to mouth, just enough to calm everyone's fraying nerves, until it was quickly emptied.

The road to hell, Djemo knew, is paved with good intentions. He lit a cigarette, offering the pack to the others, and found a piece of cardboard under the stairs to sit on. "Until all this blows over"—Pero's words kept echoing in Djemo's head. But when would it be over? Ten minutes later soldiers brought three more neighbors, Muslims, then two more, then his cousin Fudo with his son Elijan, and along with him, Djemo's own son Ari, who at sixteen looked older than his age. Life was just beginning to open up before him. Ari was drowning in his own tears.

"Don't, son, it'll all be over in no time. You shouldn't cry, it's a shame. You're a big boy now," Djemo said, hugging him.

"I can't help it," sobbed Ari. "They killed . . . "

Djemo felt the blood freeze in his veins. He first thought of his younger son, Deni, then his wife. His face turned the color of stone. For a second he thought of running home, but that would have been impossible. "Who?" he barely uttered. "Who did they kill?"

Ari couldn't stop sobbing. Finally he turned to his father, hugged him, and said, "They killed Lando." He kept crying as he said, "They pumped a whole round into him."

Djemo lit another cigarette and blew the smoke out high over everyone. When you're scared, you can dream up anything, he thought to himself. Lando was the true favorite in Djemo's family, a black Doberman, only eighteen months old, and a real beauty. Ari often took him out for walks to show him off to his friends or to play in the park. He had taught him to obey commands, to fetch a stick or a ball, and to dive into the water with him when they went swimming. The dog had learned to walk over a very narrow bridge across the canal and even to stand on his hind legs and put his front paws on Ari's chest and lick his face.

Djemo had loved that dog, and he was sorry that he had been killed. He tried to comfort his weeping son and promised to get another dog exactly like Lando. But he sensed that a long time would pass before he could make good on the promise.

About twenty people had gathered under the stairs, although it would have been more accurate to say

". . . had been brought" than ". . . had gathered." Pero made a list of everyone and asked them all to hand over their money and other valuables to him for safekeeping, promising that everything would be returned once this was over. His neighbors forked everything over; they trusted him.

An hour or so later Pero asked Djemo to step outside, saying that Bato Kovačević, a policeman whom Djemo knew very well, wanted him. Outside Djemo found himself facing the barrel of an automatic rifle. Bato ordered him to put his hands behind his head and steered him toward a paddy wagon parked at the other end of the building. On his way there, at every entrance of the building, Djemo saw his Serb neighbors, each armed with various weapons. Bato simply dumped him into the back of the wagon and locked the door. Emir, Redžo, Mujo, and a few other neighbors were already inside. The wagon had no windows, so they didn't know where they were being taken.

After a few minutes on the road the paddy wagon stopped. The back door was opened, and they got out. They were near the police station. A lot of armed policemen stood around, accompanied by masked soldiers in fatigues. The smell of burning kerosene filled the air, along with the clatter of a generator. They were ordered to raise their arms and stand against the wall with their legs apart. Then a policeman approached and, cursing all the while, began to search them, the way hardened criminals are searched in the movies. In one of his pockets Djemo had a pack of cigarettes and a lighter, in the other pocket some money and his ID. The policeman took away his lighter and cigarettes and gave him back the money and the ID card.

The men were forced to stand against the wall for about half an hour, in the same position, taking in the curses along with an occasional blow to the back with a rifle butt. The sun was beating down on them without mercy. At one point Djemo thought he couldn't take it anymore, that he would collapse. He felt dizzy; objects flickered before his eyes; one of his knees buckled, and down he went. A soldier came over, hoisted him up by the armpit, and offered him a can of beer. "Have a drink, you'll feel better," he said. Djemo took a couple of swigs and did feel better. He put the can down on a ledge of the wall he was leaning against and thanked the soldier without looking at him. He didn't dare turn, even though he very much wanted to know who had helped him.

Later the soldiers took them upstairs two by two, and the ones remaining could hear the sounds of beating and cursing and the screams of those being beaten. The time came for Djemo and another guy to go upstairs. A skinny young man with a big beard walked in front of Djemo up the stairs, along which, about one yard apart, heavily armed soldiers and policemen stood. Djemo saw that each held a club in his hand, rubber, plastic, or wood. But they didn't hit him.

When Djemo and his companion got to the door leading to the canteen, one of the policemen told Djemo to wait while he took the other guy inside. The door was left ajar. Djemo could see everything. They began hitting the guy, using clubs, feet, fists, and whatever else they could find. "You motherfucker," they cursed, beating on him without letup. "We're protecting you, you and your family, and you shoot at us. You had a gunner's nest on top of your house." And they beat him harder.

The man swore by his very eyes, by all that was dear to him, by his children, that he had no weapons, neither he nor anyone else in the family, but that didn't help him at all; they just kept beating him. A trail of blood began trickling down from above his right eye. Eventually the soldiers threw him out the door, where Djemo stood mutely, and the uniformed men on the stairs hit the poor guy some more as they dragged him downstairs. Then Djemo's turn came.

One of the soldiers motioned him to come in. He took two or three steps, just enough to find himself surrounded by the raging beasts. He was taken aback when, instead of a beating, he got a request: "And now tell us all you know about the attack and where you were while it was going on." Djemo thought hard. What should he say? That he didn't know a thing? They wouldn't believe that he'd only heard about the attack on the radio. But there wasn't enough time to think things through. "Since the shooting at Hambarine," he said, "I haven't been away from my family, from my house. I listened to the instructions given out by the Emergency Committee on the radio and did everything they said until the soldiers came and brought me here"—all of this in a single breath. He pulled his head in toward his shoulders a little, waiting for their reaction. A powerful fear that he had never felt before coursed through his entire body.

"This one's loyal," a voice behind him could be heard. "I know him. He worked at the radio station." And then the owner of that voice of salvation came around to face him. Djemo didn't know him, but he understood that the few emblems on his epaulets made him the master of the present situation.

"And do you know which of your neighbors had weapons?" he asked. "Believe me, I don't," said Djemo, addressing only the one with the emblems on his epaulets. "I was never interested in what my neighbors had or didn't have or what they did. I didn't even know a lot of them." He was aware of the absolute hopelessness of his position. "Take him away," replied the commander with a sneer, as he sat down on the edge of the table by the window. Djemo wasn't even beaten by those standing outside, the ones with the clubs. It was as if they had gotten a secret signal.

At the time Djemo had no idea that he had passed into the first circle of hell.

Chapter Two

Later that afternoon the prisoners were loaded onto a bus, from which waved a big Serbian flag mounted on one of the side mirrors. Three soldiers sat in the front seats facing them. The bus started moving. It went straight to the underpass, then right, then left toward the cellulose and paper factory, before turning down the street running along the banks of the Sana River. Djemo looked at the Old City. Tongues of flame rose high above the burning roofs. Dense whirls of smoke gathered into huge black clouds.

The Old City, that island in the river surrounded by the Sana and the Berek, looked like an enormous torch. "That's how all your houses will burn," said one of the soldiers.

Djemo just kept quiet, impotently gritting his teeth and sighing in despair, feeling almost unbearably humiliated. It seemed to him that he would remember this image of the Old City in flames until his dying day. That part of the city was the source of many sweet memories. He fell in love for the first time right there, on the banks of the Berek, and it was there that he smoked his first cigarette. The dances held on the stage of the open-air theater were unforgettable, not only for the people of Prijedor but for those from other places who came to spend the summer. And swimming at night in the Sana . . . memories kept reeling as his throat tightened. And the misery flowed from his eyes. His body felt weighed down by helplessness and humiliation. He reached toward his pocket for a cigarette but remembered that his cigarettes had been taken away at the police station.

Their heads bent down, their eyes bereft of hope, the prisoners lurched forward as the bus led them into the unknown. The Serb soldiers in the front of the bus occasionally greeted passersby with three raised fingers in the traditional Serb salute; they also sang some strange, unintelligible songs. One group of villagers in fatigues and muddy boots signaled to the bus driver to stop. They asked the escorting soldiers to hand over the prisoners. Looking over the frightened men on the bus, one villager said, "Those are *Ustasha*"—the Croatian fascists who collaborated with Hitler in World War II. "They should all be taken care of using the 'shortcut,'" he said, holding his hand like a knife across his neck, his face twisting in an eerie grimace of hate. He and his friends were ready to lynch the prisoners on the spot, though they didn't know any of them.

One of the soldiers mumbled something and ordered the driver to shut the door and drive on. Through the window Djemo could see the wide expanse of the plain at the foot of the Kozara Mountains, just where the turf of tilled soil reached its highest elevation. Fertile, plowed land, sown with wheat, extending as far as the eye could see. "Who will harvest it?" wondered Djemo. Abandoned cattle, cows, horses, sheep, and newborn lambs grazed in the fields. They wandered around scorched houses as long spits of flame and pillars of smoke soared high above them. In front of the houses, fresh linen still hung on lines stretched across the court-yards. No one had expected such evil.

Djemo remembered the words of the great novelist Ivo Andrić: "Only in the Balkans can anything happen anytime." And it had happened, the worst that can happen, right here by the mountain range, where history marches in military step. In the Kozara Mountains people had always started again from scratch, after every battle, after every plague. The mountain people were tough, but it was also true that no one could love their patch of sky, their fields and houses and mountains, as much as they did.

In earlier wars the locals had fought to defend Bosnia's border region from various enemies, but now . . . what exactly was happening now? Who were these mighty warriors who fled their farms, leaving behind half-empty beer bottles, to take up cannons and machine guns, to fire mortars and bullets, heedless of what they aimed at or how many rounds they shot? Once, not so long ago, people had made sacrifices; they had gone without food for the greater good. Now they were defying the legal authorities to arm what had once been everyone's army, the Yugoslav People's Army, taking refuge in the five-pointed star and the attribute "People's." And now that army was pounding Bosnians with the very same weapons they had acquired to defend themselves from any possible enemy—only the enemy, it turned out, had been living right next door, right down the street. Until just yesterday Bosnians had shared everything, drinking coffee together, going to parties and funerals together, visiting each other, marrying each other, but now . . .

To the old song's words "Where the People's Army marches . . . ," Djemo would have added ". . . is a land where grass no longer grows." These were strange times. Bosnia trembled as if it had been hit by a powerful earthquake. But an earthquake comes and goes. This upheaval just kept on coming.

Was this bus trip the beginning of something still worse? The people beaten up—what were they guilty of? And what about the others, staring at the floor of the bus, their eyes filled with fear? The new Serbian authorities had nothing to blame them for, other than that their very existence was a reminder that Bosnia had long been home to Muslims and Croats as well as Serbs. Now Serbs were destroying mosques and churches and even digging up graveyards. Such crimes were well organized and harked back to times everyone thought had been forgotten. Irrational hatred flowed from the darkest parts of their souls and stared out from their bloodshot eyes. The reaction of most people was silence, fearful silence.

The bus stopped outside the administration building of the iron ore mine at Omarska, only a few miles from the village of the same name. On one side, looted cattle grazed in the mowed fields, while across from them the mining embankments—busy with workers until only days before—lay remote and isolated, seared by the unbearable heat. Two huge buildings stood in the center, separated by a wide asphalt lot with two smaller buildings. The prisoners were ordered to get off the bus with their arms raised over their heads, holding up three fingers on each hand. Two rows of fully armed soldiers opened a path through which they had to walk. Five men were pulled out of the line; the others were taken into one of the big buildings. Among the five selected, Djemo recognized Tewfik, a local actor whom everyone called "Cheapskate." Within minutes a burst of machine-gun fire rang out. Cheapskate would never "break a leg" on stage again.

With every arriving busload, the room got more and more crowded. Djemo's son arrived, along with his cousins Fadil, Mirsad, and Fudo, and Fudo's son Elijan. By Djemo's count, over twenty buses arrived before dark.

The pattern repeated itself the next day. Over the course of two days more than three thousand inhabitants of Prijedor and its outlying villages were arrested in their homes in these inconceivable raids and brought to the Serb prison at Omarska. Among the prisoners, whose only fault was being Muslim or Croat, were intellectuals, teachers, engineers, police officers, craftsmen. Djemo recognized the mayor of Prijedor, the Honorable Mr. Muhamed Čehajić. How absurd such a title seemed now.

The prisoners were given nothing to eat for the first four days. They slept on a tiled floor. Djemo found a cardboard box, broke it up, and put it on the floor for himself and his son to use as a bed. The stale air was hard to breathe and dried out their throats. On the fifth day they were ordered to line up for food. Their hunger was unbearable. Everyone swarmed to the door, and they were taken away in groups of thirty. Ari was in the third group; Djemo was way back in the tenth. When Djemo's group came up, they were told there was no more food. They went back to their places, writhing in pain. Later all prisoners would be given food once a day: a couple of cabbage leaves with a few beans, covered in tepid water, and a piece of bread that seemed to be made of soapsuds. They would be allowed only two minutes to eat.

Most of the time the prisoners were beaten on the way to and from the canteen where they ate. That route wound through a narrow corridor that branched off at the end and led to a staircase on the right. Upstairs, prisoners were interrogated. Back downstairs, on the left, was the canteen. The guards would pour water on a worn-out patch of glazed cement to make the corridor more slippery. If a prisoner fell, the guards would pounce on him like famished beasts at the sight of a carcass. Using whips made of thick electrical cable, they beat the fallen prisoner all the way up the stairs for the inevitable interrogation—or simply to finish the job they had already started.

In the presence of the interrogators—inspectors from the Prijedor police station—the guards would strike the prisoner with shoes, brass knuckles, iron rods, and God knows what else in order to force an admission of guilt and get a signature on a trumped-up confession. Usually they got the prisoner to admit that he had taken part in attacks on Prijedor, or carried arms, or been found with lists of Serbs to be liquidated by Muslims. These false accounts were taken as evidence warranting the use of force and torture. The goal was clear: to eliminate in each man any hope of survival.

A young doctor from Kozarac, Mensur Kusuran, was forced to confess that he had stolen medicine from the clinic where he worked, hid it in his cellar, and then smuggled it to Muslims. Mensur, of course, had no clue as to what any of this was about. He swore that he had never taken a single dose of medicine from the clinic, but to no avail. After being forced to sign the confession that sealed his fate, Mensur remembered that his house had no cellar. The interrogators just laughed and told the guard to take him away. (Of the many doctors who would pass through the camp at Omarska, Mensur was the only one known to survive its horrors.)

Similarly, Eso Mehmedagić, a prominent public figure from Prijedor, was accused of being a sniper. It didn't seem to matter that, as everyone knew, Eso was afflicted with progressive blindness. He couldn't even walk down the street without help.

About six hundred prisoners were being held in Djemo's dorm. The space wasn't very big; it had once been the miners' locker room. The youngest inmate was just fourteen, a boy from the village of Bišćani, whose entire family had been killed. The oldest was seventy-four, Uncle Gredelj from Čejrek, another village outside Prijedor.

Only a wall separated these six hundred prisoners from a small garage. No more than about ninety square feet, the garage was occupied by 160 people from Kozarac, a small town with a largely Muslim population about fifteen miles from Prijedor. They had put up the longest resistance to the Serbs, so the guards showed them no mercy. These 160 prisoners had been captured somewhere near Benkovac, on Mount Kozara. Most were armed, but unable to mount a stronger resistance, they had finally surrendered. Hadn't they heard on the radio that those who gave up their weapons would be guaranteed complete safety? They were certainly "safe" in the small garage, in their torn clothes, standing barefoot on the concrete floor.

It was horrifying to listen to their screams, their cries for help. The days were hot, the nights muggy and oppressive, as only they can be in these parts. The men would ask the guards for water. Through a high broken window the guards tossed in a plastic water canister every now and then, and the men would struggle frantically to get even a few drops of water, a matter of life and death. Since they fought over the canister, more water was spilled than reached their parched throats. Some turned the empty canister upside down and shook it above their gaping mouths, hoping for the very last drop.

The guards snickered and promised more water, but only if the prisoners would sing the songs of the Serbian nationalists, the *chetnik* songs. They had to sing— songs like this one:

You say Serbia's small
Liars one and all!
She's not small at all,

Not small at all.
Thrice she went
To battle, from Topola
All the way to Ravna Gora;
And everywhere you go
The loyal guards
Everywhere you go
The loyal guards
Of our General Draža . . .

Oh Alija, oh Alija,
If we go to battle
It's you I'll kill,
You I'll slaughter,
Just like Miloš once
Got rid of Murat . . .

See the Turk at her Mosque bowing,
Her love to Serbs only swearing . . .

"Louder," the guards would say, "louder, if you want more water." And the chorus of the afflicted rose. "Once more and you'll get water." The guards laughed. "Louder, take it from the top!" The wretched prisoners sang for hours, hoping for at least some relief from the unbearable thirst brought on by the sweltering night.

The prisoners took care of their bodily needs using a plastic bucket by the tin door of the garage. When somebody took a leak, the others gathered around to cup their hands and catch the urine, wetting their chapped lips with it and even drinking it. They slept standing up, because there was no space to lie down. Those next to the wall raised their hands high above their heads, keeping them against the wall; paint ran under their palms from the heat and moisture, trickling down their arms to create hideous reliefs.

Once, for no reason at all, a drunken guard let go a burst of machine-gun fire at the garage door. Djemo and his fellow prisoners could hear screams and cries for help. Word spread that one prisoner in the garage had been killed and four seriously wounded. The four were taken somewhere, supposedly to a hospital, but nobody saw them again.

One time Djemo caught sight of the miserable prisoners in the garage through the wide door to his area. A group of about ten of them were chosen and taken out some forty yards in front of the garage. They were ordered to undress completely. The prisoners began taking off their worn, ragged clothes and putting them in a pile as four guards looked on. The guards were completely drunk, as anyone could tell by the way they moved. As the prisoners stripped, bashfully using their hands to try to cover their nakedness, the guards fixed their cynical glares upon them even more intently.

One big man, over six feet tall, refused to strip. His beard was long, a sign that he had been imprisoned for quite some time. He simply kept quiet and didn't move. He stood with his head bowed, mutely watching. One of the guards came up to him, put the barrel of his rifle to the man's neck, and said something to him. The man just stood there, without moving a single part of his body. "The poor guy's going to get it, they'll kill him," said someone behind Djemo. Djemo didn't turn around or respond but kept looking through the upper part of the glass door that separated the inmates from the guards. He was watching to see what would happen to this defiant figure and the other men from Kozarac.

The guard, seeing that the man was steadfast in his intention not to carry out the order, aimed his rifle upward and fired several shots into the air. Except for some quail in a nearby tree flying away out of sight, nothing happened. The man stood stubbornly in place without making the slightest movement. While bluish smoke still rose from the rifle barrel, the guard struck the clothed man in the middle of the head with the rifle butt, once and then again, until the man fell. Then the guard handed his rifle to another guard and moved his hand to his belt. A knife flashed in his hand, a long army knife.

He bent down, grabbing hold of the poor guy's hair with his free hand. Another guard joined in, continuously cursing. He, too, had a flashing knife in his hand. The two other guards backed off a little and trained their rifles on the nine naked prisoners, observing their every move. The guards with the knives started using them to tear away the man's clothes. After only a few seconds, they stood up, their own clothes covered with blood. The air resounded with a long, loud, and painful wail. It sent shivers through all who heard it.

Never in all his life was Djemo to see a more horrifying sight. The poor man stood up a little, or rather tried to stand up, still letting out excruciating screams.

He was covered with blood. One guard took a water hose from a nearby hydrant and directed the strong jet at the poor prisoner. A mixture of blood and water flowed down his exhausted, gaunt, naked body as he bent down repeatedly, like a wounded Cyclops, raising his arms above his head, then lowering them toward the jet of water to fend it off; his cries were those of someone driven to insanity by pain. And then Djemo, and everyone else, saw clearly what had happened: the guards had cut off the man's sexual organ and half of his behind.

After that Djemo couldn't remember anything. The shocking sight of that horror momentarily numbed his mind. Only later was he told that the poor man, after succumbing to the torture, was taken to a garbage container, doused with gasoline, and burned. The other men were taken back to the garage.

When the interrogations began, the garage gradually started to empty. Eventually no more than fifty people were left, living witnesses to incarceration in the infamous garage.

A constant fear permeated the prisoners' very bones, spreading throughout their bodies. It took great stoicism to endure the contempt and torture. Days went by, one day like the one before, and each day even more like the one that followed. Hot, humid days followed by rain, then more rain followed by heat and humidity. Frail bodies became even frailer. The pale faces bore expressions of immeasurable suffering, irretrievable loss of peace of mind, and human dignity devastated beyond repair. Movement around the already tight space was reduced to a minimum in order to save energy. Lined up along the walls on their cardboard beds in their ragged sweaters and jackets, the men, looking as if they had been cemented into the darkness, talked less and less. They believed that they were saving their energy, forgetting for the time the offenses fate had inflicted on them. They knew that they had to get to the other side of the abyss. Their beards were growing, and their unkempt hair turning gray.

Who could have remembered the need for a hair-brush under such circumstances? They needed brushes, however, not to stay neat and stylish but to combat a new affliction that had come to plague them. Since the prisoners had no way to wash or take baths, they became infested with lice. At first they removed the lice and shyly, so that no one would see, squeezed them to death between their fingernails. Later the lice simply dropped every time they moved their heads. The prisoners looked through each other's hair to find the parasites and kill them. They would say: "On top of the ones over there, another enemy's come to the front." Soon the lice had infested their ragged clothing as well.

Nights were the hardest to bear and seemed to last forever. Misery and helplessness weighed heavily on the prisoners as they scratched their heads, their armpits, their entire bodies, their empty stomachs.

Chapter Three

Shots from outside. Screaming and the sound of beatings. Then the nightly roll calls. It was hard to say whether life had anything worse to offer.

In the wee hours of the night, always well past midnight, one of the guards—hitting whoever happened to be closest to the door—would break the silence: "Everybody up!" Whoever happened to be woken up by the guard roused his neighbors, each in turn, until everybody was up. Then the guard called out the first and last names of one or more prisoners, who were then ordered to go out with him. They were returned within half an hour or an hour, dumped through the door like sacks, bloody and beaten, often with broken arms or legs. Sometimes the broken bones were even visible. Whoever was close by tried to help as much as possible, putting wet rags on the bruises or bandaging arms and legs with pieces of torn shirts and underwear; the prisoners even ripped plywood off the door to use as splints. Images of these nighttime beatings left indelible scars on the psyches of the prisoners. They became mute and withdrew further into themselves.

Later Dr. Eso Sadiković was brought to Djemo's dorm. He was a distinguished ear, nose, and throat specialist, chief of the otolaryngology staff at the Prijedor hospital. Everyone in Prijedor knew and liked him, both for his professional ability and his willingness to help anyone, whether a lifelong or first-time patient. Dr. Sadiković worked as a consultant for the United Nations all over the world but had come back to Prijedor, the town he loved so dearly, a few years ago. Before the events recounted here began to unfold, he had often spoken on the radio, calling upon his fellow citizens to opt for peace, mutual respect, and understanding. The Serb authorities now "understood" him best of all: he was arrested in his own house and brought to the Omarska camp.

Yet Dr. Sadiković remained willing to help anyone anytime, both in and out of the camp. Even the guards called on his medical expertise since, in their utter ineptitude, they often wounded themselves. They kept the safety off their guns and, with their itchy trigger fingers, sometimes discharged their rifles by accident. Most of the time they shot themselves in the foot or the leg, since they slung their weapons over their shoulders upside down. Dr. Sadiković was given bandages and anything else he needed to tend to the wounded guards, while the prisoners got nothing. Not a thing.

Once Djemo watched Dr. Sadiković sew up a wound on a prisoner's head; it had been bashed in by a guard with an iron rod on the way to the canteen. Blood had gushed all over. As he sewed the wound up, Dr. Sadiković explained that there was more blood in the head than in any other part of the body. He used a plain sewing needle and regular tailor's thread since that was all he could get. The poor man clenched his teeth as he endured the pain of several stitches.

The doctor also helped prisoners from the other dorms at Omarska, as well as the women imprisoned there, numbering about forty altogether. Among them were two Serb women arrested for protesting the behavior of Serb soldiers and reservists toward their neighbors. One of the two was Djemo's neighbor Jovanka, who had lived in his building, the very building from whose entrance he and his neighbors had been brought to the camp.

The women slept upstairs, in the loft over Djemo's dorm; the loft was also used by the interrogation squads, who usually left early in the evening and came back around eight o'clock in the morning. During the day, while interrogations took place, the women were taken to the kitchen. Some helped ladle out food or wash the dishes, but most of them just sat in the canteen all day long, silently watching the other prisoners being abused as they ate. Djemo noticed that several times Jovanka secretly slipped something extra into Ari's hand as he left the canteen with his group. Usually it was a slice of bread, but once she even gave him a piece of chocolate. Djemo thanked his old neighbor with a slight nod.

Nuska, a judge at the municipal court, was also among the women prisoners, as well as Biba the dentist, Jadranka the journalist, and many others Djemo didn't know as well. One of the women had two sons, Elvis and Enes, in Djemo's dorm, and she often passed food secretly to them. Sometimes one of the more lenient guards let her put a bit more food in her sons' dishes or give them bigger slices of bread.

A woman by the name of Hajra was taken to the White House, where she stayed in the same room with some fifty other prisoners. The White House—what a name for a torture chamber, the place where some of the worst atrocities at the camp were committed. Its facade was indeed white. It was right next to the kitchen and had four medium-size rooms and a toilet only the guards could use. Its inmates were taken outside to relieve themselves in the field. The guards took them out in groups of four or five, or sometimes one by one. Many paid with their lives for needing to attend to their bodily needs.

One rainy night the name Mehmedalija Sarajlić was called out. A distinguished, gray-haired man about sixty years old, he was taken outside and forced to strip naked; then the guards brought him, still naked, back into the room with Hajra, a girl who couldn't have been older than twenty-two or twenty-three. She, too, was forced to strip, and they were ordered to make love in front of all the other prisoners, who looked on in horror and silence, deeply humiliated by the utter powerlessness of the man and woman before them. Mehmedalija begged, beseeching the guards, telling them that the girl could have been his granddaughter. The guards laughed cynically, like cannibals. "Oh, look who's being choosy. We don't have anybody younger at the moment. If she was good enough for us, why wouldn't she be good enough for you?"

The girl just kept trying modestly to cover herself with her hands as she begged the guards to let her put on her clothes. "Oh, no," one of them said, shamelessly flashing a toothy grin, "he'll agree to do it, for sure he will. Take him outside, in the rain," he commanded the other guards, "and bring him back only when he agrees." Mehmedalija was brought back naked after being in the rain for two hours. It was the kind of night no one would want to be out in, even properly dressed, much less the way he was. He refused again. They started beating him with rifle butts and boots. He fell down. "Throw the scum out!" one of the guards thundered. Mehmedalija was taken out on the lawn, to the right of the entrance, and left there. The next morning he was dead.

The most notorious torturer in the White House was a soldier by the name of Zoka. He boasted that he was the strongest Serb soldier in the entire Serbian army. He often carried a strip of lath, about three feet long, with a big nail hammered into one end. The sharp end of the nail stuck several inches out of the strip of lath, and he would walk around beating people with it. He'd come up to a prisoner, getting right in his face, and ask, "Which of your eyes do you like better?" With others, he'd look down: "Which ball . . . ?" He hammered another, shorter strip of lath into a young prisoner's heel and threatened to kill him if he tried to pull it out. Several days later the young man died in excruciating pain.

Seizing money, watches, and other valuables from the prisoners was part of the guards' daily routine, not only in the White House but in all the dorms, of which there were at least ten. Having their cigarettes taken away by the guards was even worse for some of the prisoners than having their food taken away. A guard would come in and say, quite simply, "Better collect two hundred German marks in ten minutes, or I'll shoot the first ten prisoners by the door." And he'd leave without giving anyone a chance to answer or explain that no one had any money, that all their money had already been taken away from them. Then the prisoners would turn their pockets inside out, removing everything they had to hand over to the prisoner chosen to collect the money. Usually the total was a lot less than had been ordered. On his return, the guard would demand five or six wristwatches, preferably Seikos.

Many guards had helpers among the prisoners who sold cigarettes and biscuits to the other prisoners at ten times the going rate. Sometimes a guard would give a carton of cigarettes to a prisoner and tell him he had to sell it at a certain price. Ten minutes later another guard would just "happen" to walk in and grab the cigarettes. Less than an hour later the first guard would come back and, pretending not to know what had gone on, ask the prisoner for his cut of money for the cigarettes. No explanation sufficed to save such a prisoner from a brutal beating.

Cigarettes were a story of their own at Omarska. Diehard smokers who had run out of cigarettes roamed around looking for other smokers, begging them for "just one puff." Sometimes ten people would smoke a single cigarette, passing it from hand to hand and mouth to mouth. Everyone would take a puff or two, getting angry at anyone who took a longer drag. Some even walked around with their mouths wide open, trying to inhale smoke that others had exhaled. Sometimes no one in the dorm had a single cigarette. Then the prisoners would put two fingers together, bring them to their lips, and breathing in as if they were smoking, "exhale."

Prisoners would collect tiny cigarette butts, no bigger than a fraction of an inch, and with consummate skill try to finish smoking them without burning themselves. Or they would take the tobacco out, wrap it in a piece of old newspaper, and smoke that. Later, when the guards started letting the prisoners out of their dorms under heavy guard, the prisoners would pick ordinary grass, dry it in the sun, wrap it, and smoke it.

In Djemo's dorm, Mujo Crnalić, a young man with an athletic build, sold the most cigarettes and biscuits. As a result, prisoners from other dorms started calling it "Mujo's dorm." It was Mujo who counted his fellow prisoners every day and lined them up for the meal. He was often given a hand by Burho Kapetanović, who had worked in the Omarska mine until shortly before being imprisoned. The guards frequently called for Mujo at night. He would get up reluctantly, put some more clothes on, and go out with the guards. Soon he would return carrying a few boxes of biscuits and packs of cigarettes, which he'd start selling to the prisoners. Several times Muharem Murselović Mursel, the well-known restaurant owner, bought cigarettes and biscuits from Mujo only to hand them out to his fellow prisoners. It was quite something to see those hungry, frantic eyes follow the biscuits and cigarettes in Mujo's hands.

Mujo would address a guard as "Comrade Sergeant," a form used by other prisoners as well on those rare occasions when they were speaking to a guard who seemed more kindly disposed. One incredibly humid night, sometime after midnight, one of the "sergeants" called for Mujo. The athletically built Mujo, with his broad shoulders, casually put on his T-shirt and went out. He never came back again.

For the next several days Burho took his place. He was also called out one night, and he, too, never came back. Burho's brother Mehmedalija, manager of a catering enterprise in Prijedor, was another prisoner who never came back from a night call. Ziko Crnalić, owner of a restaurant, disappeared together with his son Armin. Zlaja Beširović, the director of the Bosnamontaža enterprise from Prijedor, never came back; nor did Asaf Kapetanović, owner of the most popular café in Prijedor, or Nedžad Šerić, president of the Prijedor Court of Justice. Four doctors—Jusuf Pašić, Rufad Suljanović, Osman Mahmuljin, and Željko Sikora—never came back.

Only one day before the Omarska camp was closed, Dr. Eso Sadiković was called out at night. He picked up his things, all contained in a little plastic bag, and stepped quietly into the night. Those near the door saw him get into a military vehicle. At the same time two busloads carrying two hundred prisoners left the camp; they had been brought in only a few hours earlier from the Keraterm camp, which was right in town and had been emptied just that day. Those two hundred, at least according to the guards, had been Keraterm's "toughest cases." The fact that Dr. Sadiković was put in a military vehicle, not on the bus with the others, provided a glimmer of hope that he would be heard from again someday. His wife, daughter, and son remained at home, in Prijedor.

Everybody kept quiet. Silence was the only thing not forbidden in the camp. It expressed the true hideousness of existence there and the unbearable sadness of desperately trying to forget all the misery, at least for a moment. Djemo would sigh deeply and look longingly at the blue sky in the distance. "My Prijedor is over there," he would say in a loud whisper, as if to himself, and then add: "Will I ever see it again?" A well of tears would start flowing down his face. "They can't exterminate us all," someone said softly so the guards wouldn't hear. "Someone will make it, to witness their evil atrocities. Wherever wolves feast, they leave a bloody trail. They defiled Mount Kozara, and desecrated her valleys. No one, not even God, can pardon them for this."

Some nights, during a brief period of sleep, a prisoner would suddenly wake up and start raving, screaming. Once, just before dawn, as silence reigned in the room they slept in, someone shouted at the top of his lungs: "Friends, we are all living corpses!" It was Hadjo, an alcoholic who'd been on the wagon, a retired firefighter and a very kind and honest man. Later they calmed him down, but Hadjo's words rang in everyone's ears for a long time. Once, when they were returning to their dorms from the canteen in single file, Hadjo kept walking out into the field. One of the guards lifted his rifle, aimed at him, and pulled the trigger. Hadjo stumbled and fell. We found out later that he'd been shot in the shoulder but remained alive. Quite often a guard would say, "If something doesn't suit you here in the camp, just go on out into the field. We'll take care of the rest."

One day the guards took all the prisoners out to the runway. The infirm and the beaten, everyone. The prisoners helped each other stand up straight as they dragged themselves out to the runway. There were about three thousand of them. The guards forced them to stand as close as possible to the wall of the hangar, opposite the building with the kitchen and the interrogation rooms. They clung to each other under a mercilessly scorching sun. The soldiers positioned themselves around the prisoners, ready to fire. One guard, known for never parting from his machine gun for even a second, climbed to the roof of the building across the way and began loading the magazine of his gun with cartridges. When he had finished, he aimed the barrel at the runway and lay down next to it, taking aim at the men.

Djemo held Ari close, hugging him tightly. He sheltered his son's head under his arm, trying to divert his eyes from the guards around them. Two armored trucks with three long barrels aimed straight at them drove up to within several yards of the prisoners. "They're going to kill us all off," someone said. Everyone was terrified, their faces pale, their eyes full of fear but also an odd defiance. They looked straight at the guns facing them and kept quiet. The guards kept their guns trained on the prisoners for over an hour. Then they were all taken back to the dorms.

The guards were all young men from the surrounding villages: Omarska, Marićka, Gradina. They were Serb volunteers; there were no regular soldiers among them. On weekends regular troops from Banja Luka came to the camp. The guards called them specialists, and they were indeed specialists at breaking arms and legs, tearing out organs, and smashing skulls against walls. The weekends at Omarska were orgies of blood. One day, while pacing around a group of prisoners who had been taken out to the runway, one of the regulars said, loudly, so everyone could hear: "Today is my twenty-fifth birthday, and I've only killed twenty-three Muslims."

The runway was where the prisoners were brought after their meal. Men from each group coming out of the canteen would be forced to sit down there, facing away from the entrance to the canteen and the interrogation rooms. When the guards brought new prisoners from other dorms upstairs for questioning, they ordered everyone on the runway to lie on their stomachs and put their heads into their folded arms so they couldn't see sideways. That's when the guards carried out the "disobedient" ones, all broken up and sometimes even dead, to be loaded onto a yellow van and taken away. Most of the time other prisoners loaded the corpses onto the van; usually they too ended up as corpses on the same van, to eliminate the possibility of leaving living witnesses. With the scorching sun above frying the asphalt below, it wasn't at all unusual for the prisoners to stay on their stomachs on the runway for up to ten hours, especially on days when the guards had been particularly "efficient." This ritual happened almost every day.

On rare occasions, the prisoners were allowed to walk around the runway or sit wherever they wanted, but always under the watchful eyes of the guards. Once, as the men let their guard down and relaxed a little after their meal, Rizo Hadžalić, a man in his early thirties, joined Djemo's group. He was sitting and eating a piece of bread he hadn't managed to finish in the canteen because the guard, as usual, had hurried them on. A soldier came by and, with a devious smile, said, "Cheers!" Rizo looked at him, and for just an instant the soldier seemed friendly, almost a nice guy. Rizo responded in the traditional Bosnian way, with a hearty "Bujrum," meaning "Thanks."

"You think you can just say 'Bujrum' to me, you motherfucker? Well, now let me introduce you to God!"

The "nice guy" suddenly turned into a ferocious beast. He grabbed Rizo and, clubbing him with his truncheon, took him upstairs. A few minutes later he called two prisoners from the runway to come upstairs and carry Rizo down to the runway, ordering the others to lie on their stomachs. Rizo's bitter crying could be heard on the runway, but nobody dared make the slightest move, let alone try to help him. His sobbing became softer and softer. "Take the scum inside," commanded one of the guards. When the prisoners stood up to go to the dorm, Rizo was the only one left on the runway. He was dead.

Later Rizo's wife was brought to the camp. No one dared tell her what had happened. The guards, of course, didn't have the courage to look the woman in the eye and tell her, "We killed your husband," even though each gesture they made said as much. Nor could they offer a single word to justify what they had done. Rizo was a peaceful guy, a model citizen, and above all, a great father. His children, still in Prijedor, wouldn't learn of their father's death for a long time to come. His wife sat in the same chair in the canteen day after day, facing the runway, resting her chin in her palm. She was searching for something, her eyes filled with mistrust and doubt, almost as if she knew the truth.

The souls of those on the inside whom the beasts outside hadn't yet devoured bore the same marks. Fate had been anything but generous to them. Their bodies looked as if they had risen from the grave even as the earth still came thudding down against the planks above them. Beating and cursing, cursing and beating, and constant humiliation, the most painful wound that can be inflicted on a human being. It was as if even the slightest kindness had been put under lock and key.

The Serb jailers—treading on their own promises with combat boots and piercing them with daggers, for no benefit to themselves or their tribe—were playing some strange game. But in that game, prisoners perished. The game was becoming a way of life, a daily routine. Anyone in his right mind knew that a game starting out with such low odds couldn't end well.

And where on earth was the poisonous game conceived? In the head of that bloodthirsty lyricist, the mad psychiatrist from Sarajevo, Radovan Karadžić. Years before, clearly spelling out the evil to come, he had written: "Take no pity let's go / kill that scum down in the city." It was he who formed the sham government, a shadow of the powers centered in Belgrade. It was he who roused Serbs to a hatred that they used to fortify the dim byways of their souls, invigorating them with violent, merciless, and implacable power. Would they ever sober up from their intoxicated, anything but naive revelry?

The prisoners—seized against their will and humiliated at every turn, the smiles gone forever from their withered lips, exhausted and sick, starving to death, staring absently with glassy eyes—were made of the same substance, were born under the same sky, and had lived on the same soil as their jailers. "And so it came to pass in a country of peasants, in the hilly Balkans," as the old poetess said. The prisoners didn't even know which country they lived in anymore. Every one of them would have said Bosnia-Herzegovina. But their jailers claimed it was the "Serb Republic." Of course, the prisoners would agree that it was a republic of Serbs—then add that it was also a republic of Muslims,

Croats, and everyone else who lived there. People had always lived in this country together, for centuries.

"And so it came to pass in a country of peasants, in the hilly Balkans." This was a land of peasants and tough mountainfolk, a land filled with the aroma of handmade moccasins and freshly plowed virgin soil. A land of shiny shoes and shish kebab and olive oil and suntan lotion on naked bodies bronzed in the heat, down on the Adriatic. Of incomparable ballads—"Oh Bosnia, so tender and fine . . . "—and bitter foreboding: "Oh Bosnia, my land, my wasted beauty. . . . "

Chapter Four

Wednesday, June 10, early evening. The interrogators had already left for the day, in the van that took them back and forth from Prijedor. One of the guards, drunker than usual, stuck his unkempt head through the door of the dorm and called for Djemo.

The same deathly silence that accompanied night calls descended on the dorm. Djemo felt a booming in his head, as if hundreds of hammers were pounding at his temples, at the top of his skull and the nape of his neck. His heart started pounding wildly; he could feel it beating in every part of his body. His blood pulsed through the labyrinth of capillaries across his face. He turned to his son and began to speak, his voice breaking: "Don't be scared, son, nothing will happen to me." Djemo hugged Ari tightly, feeling the delicate, rhythmic trembling of his fragile body.

"Ari, son, Daddy will be back, believe me." Timidly he took his son's arms off his shoulders, turned aside so that Ari wouldn't see the tears trickling down his cheeks, and started to walk away, not believing his own words. Somewhere at the back of his head he could almost feel the eyes of the poor souls whose silence spoke so eloquently. Gasps and deep sobs began from where he had been sitting, first softly, then louder and louder. Ari was weeping as the weak arms of those nearby reached out to keep him from going after his father. "Daddy, come back, please!" Djemo stopped for a second as his eyes tracked his son's voice. Something big and heavy, like a cannonball, lodged in his throat. He could hardly breathe. The tears that had trickled down his cheeks now flowed freely. Trying to flee such a merciless fate, he forced himself to utter: "I'll be back, son, I'll be back." Then he stepped forward past the guard, whose bearded face was flushed and whose eyes transmitted only darkness.

"In front of me," the guard ordered, pointing to the White House. On the way over he ranted and raved, cursing and occasionally pounding Djemo on the back with his truncheon. The hot, heavy air made everything even more unbearable. Djemo cast one more dull glance backward, into the distance, almost stopping. The guard pushed the barrel of his rifle hard into Djemo's back, until he felt a sharp pain and beads of sweat gathered on his face.

An overwhelming desire came over Djemo. He was on the verge of turning to spit in the bearded creature's face and punch him right in the middle of his ugly, drunken snout. But no—the voice of his son resounded in his ears like a seal ripped open within his torn heart. Defiantly, Djemo raised his head high above his shoulders and kept walking. The guard took him to the White House, to the second room on the left. (There were no prisoners in the White House then; they were only brought in later.) The next second, something heavy was let loose from above, from the sky, and knocked Djemo over the head. He fell.

Something flashed across his eyes, and everything became blurry. Blistering heat scorched his face and neck. He couldn't open his eyes. Half-conscious, sensing that he had to fight to survive, he wiped the blood from his eyes and forehead and raised his head. He saw four creatures, completely drunk, like a pack of starving wolves, with clubs in their hands and unadorned hatred in their eyes. Among them was the frenzied leader of the bloodthirsty pack, Zoran Žigić, the infamous Žiga whose soul, if he had one at all, was spattered with blood. He was said to have killed over two hundred people, including many children, in the "cleansing" operations around Prijedor. He took barely enough time between slaughters to put his bloody knife back into its sheath. Scrawny and long-legged, with a big black scar on his face, Žiga seemed like an ancient devil come to visit a time as cruel as his own. Anyone who came close to him also came close to death.

"Now, then, let me show you how Žiga does it," he said, ordering Djemo to kneel down in the corner by the radiator, "on all fours, just like a dog." The maniac grinned. Djemo knelt down and leaned forward on his hands, feeling humiliated and as helpless as a newborn. Just then they brought three more prisoners in from his dorm: Asaf, Kiki, and Bego. Being the last, Bego was immediately taken to the room across the way by Nikica, the youngest of the group of murderers. The sounds of beating and screaming soon reached the room Djemo was in. Asaf had to take the same position as Djemo, only at the other end of the radiator.

The tallest of the guards, another local murderer, named Duća, ordered Kiki to lie down on his back in the middle of the room. Then he jumped as high as he could and, with all his 250-odd pounds, came crashing down on Kiki's stomach and ribs. Another wild man wearing a headband came up to Asaf and started hitting him with a truncheon made out of thick electrical cable. Žiga kept hitting Djemo the whole time on the back and head with a club that unfurled itself every time he swung it to reveal a metal ball on the end. Djemo curled up, trying to protect his head by pulling it in toward his shoulders and covering it with his right hand. Žiga just kept cursing as he hit, his eyes inflamed by more and more hatred. The first drops of blood appeared on the tiles under Djemo's head, becoming denser and denser until they formed a thick, dark red puddle. Žiga kept at it; he stopped only every now and then, exhausted by his nonstop orgy of violence, to fan himself, waving his shirttail in front of his contorted face.

At some point a man in fatigues appeared at the door. It was Šaponja, a member of the famous Bosna-montaža soccer club from Prijedor; Djemo had once known him quite well. He came up to Djemo and said, "Well, well, my old pal Djemo. While I was fighting in Pakrac and Lipik, you were pouring down the cold ones in Prijedor." He kicked Djemo right in the face with his boot. Then he kicked him again in the chest, so badly that Djemo felt like his ribs had been shattered by the weight of the heavy combat boots. He barely managed to stay up on his arms and legs, to keep himself from falling. He knew that if he fell it would be all over. Žiga laughed like a maniac. Then he pushed Šaponja away and started hitting Djemo again with his weird club, even more fiercely than before.

The strange smell of blood, sweat, and wailing that enveloped the room only increased the cruelty of the enraged beasts. Djemo received another, even stronger kick to the face. He clutched himself in pain, bent a little to one side, and collapsed, his head sinking into the now-sizable pool of blood beneath him. Žiga grabbed him by the hair, lifted his head, and looked into Djemo's completely disfigured face: "Get up, you scum, and get out, everybody out," he shouted. Pulling Djemo up by the hair, Žiga raised him to his feet. Djemo could barely stand up, but he managed to take one step and then another, with Asaf and Kiki following.

"On all fours, I said—like dogs!" Žiga bellowed, like a dictator. He forced the three men to crawl up to a puddle by the entrance to the White House and then ordered them to wash in the filthy water. Their hands trembling, they washed the blood off their faces. "The boys have been eating strawberries and got themselves a little red," said Žiga, laughing like a madman before he chased them all back into the White House. Another prisoner, Slavko Ećimović, a Croat, and one of the first to rebel against local Serb rule, was in the same room where they had just been tortured. At least, it *seemed* like him. He was kneeling, all curled up, by the radiator. When he lifted his head, where his face should have been was nothing but the bloody, spongy tissue under the skin that had just been ripped off. Instead of eyes, two hollow sockets were filled with black, coagulated blood.

"You'll all end up like this, you and your families," Žiga said, taking on the airs of a military commander. "We killed his father and mother. And his wife. We'll get his kids. And yours, too, we'll kill you all." And with a wide swing of his leg, he kicked Djemo right in the face again with his boot. Djemo felt pieces of dried blood flying out of his mouth and nose and shards of broken teeth cutting his tongue. Then everything stopped—the blows, the curses, even the screams seemed to subside. As if through a fog, Djemo saw someone in an officer's uniform enter the room. In response to some tacit command, the beating had stopped. The prisoners were taken out to be washed at the same puddle and then returned to the dorms. Slavko Ećimović stayed in the White House and was never seen again.

Djemo went first. When he opened the door to the dorm, the murmur of voices inside stopped. A hush came over the room. He held his arms out, barely able to see the people backing up in front of him to clear the way. And then a shrill scream: "Daddy!" Djemo felt his son's arms clutch him before he sank into the deepest abyss. His body was overcome by absolute dark and silence. He didn't know how much time had gone by before he heard indistinct voices and felt something cold on his face and body. He tried to open his eyes. He felt a sharp pain in his head. As wet and cold compresses were applied to his face and back, Djemo managed to notice, though only with great effort, the many people around him and the tearful face of his son.

His recovery lasted twenty days. During that time he couldn't even move. Ari and some other prisoners had to carry him to the toilet. It didn't make Djemo feel very good, having everyone else do things for him. He couldn't even get to the canteen to eat, so his mates would save up pieces of bread or an occasional biscuit, depriving themselves in order to give him something to eat. Every day Ari brought his father half of his own meal.

When Djemo looked at himself in the mirror for the first time, he started crying. His face was covered with black contusions and bruises. Where his nose had been, there was only a huge swelling that almost shut his eyes. Several of his front teeth were broken. His whole back was black and blue. The tracks of the endless blows converged into a single, dark surface that spread over his entire back and neck. Dr. Sadiković told him later that his nose, a rib, and his right hand, at the wrist, were all broken, but that he would be all right: "You've pulled through. That's the most important thing. None of us thought you'd make it. At least now I can tell you, you're tough." The doctor made splints with wood ripped off the door and bandaged them around Djemo's broken hand with strips of cloth torn from his own shirt.

Asaf was beaten again, twice. After the second time he couldn't lie down. He spent days and nights sitting in a chair and slept there, his arms resting on a partition as he leaned forward. He had to be carried to the toilet on a chair. After he got a little better, the guards called him out a third time, and he never came back.

Kiki was beaten up two more times too. He also tried to commit suicide twice. One time he tried to cut his veins with a piece of metal; another time the guards took a piece of wire off his neck that he had tried to hang himself with on the doorjamb to the toilet. The wire was used to clean the sewage pipes that were almost always backed up, emitting an unbearable stench that permeated the area.

Bego was beaten three more times by Nikica, the pretentious, rich city kid. As he beat Bego for the last time, Nikica said: "I wanted to kill you this time, but my mama asked me to spare you, so you could live. She heard you had children. I promised my mama." Afterward Bego left. We never saw him again.

Žiga and his "boys" didn't even "work" at Omarska; they were based at Keraterm. However, their criminal skills were often called for at Omarska, which was open to all Serb volunteers who had one of "their" people there—a prisoner on whom they wanted to vent their rage for one reason or another. Such prisoners were usually their next-door neighbors. These distorters of history, with their own distorted looks and grimaces that cut to the quick as surely as the knives tucked in their belts, never missed a chance to lord their power over their victims. Most prominent among them were the local small-time gangsters and petty crooks, who were particularly eager to assert themselves. Overnight

they had turned into their neighbors' inveterate enemies. It was said that anyone could give a Serb soldier
in town fifty bucks and a piece of paper with the name
of a prisoner on it, and rest assured that the prisoner
wouldn't make it through the next morning.

While recovering from Žiga's beating, a hajji from
Bosanska Kostajnica helped Djemo a lot. Hajji Ramiz
slept by Djemo's side, offering his part of the blanket,
while he himself lay on a ragged leather jacket. Hajji
Ramiz was sick. In a car accident a few months before
he had broken a few ribs as well as his right leg in a
number of places. He had been treated in the Prijedor
hospital. After recovering and being released from the
hospital, he was seized in a roundup on the street and
brought to the Omarska camp. He had a metal rod in
his broken leg and walked with a limp.

"When you go home," Hajji Ramiz told Djemo, "get
a fresh lambskin, put it over your back, and wear it for a
few days. That's the best thing for healing bruises from
a beating like that." On rainy days he used to say: "This
is God's doing. Rain must wash away all the blood from
the earth. And it won't stop until all the dead are
buried."

After Djemo had been imprisoned for two months, the Serbs released everyone under eighteen and over sixty-five. Hajji Ramiz went with them. For Djemo, it was the happiest of days: his son Ari was among those released, as was Elijan, his cousin Fudo's son. They were called out early in the morning, taken to the runway, and kept there the whole day, the sun mercilessly beating down on them. It wasn't until late afternoon that two buses arrived to take them to Trnopolje, a camp the Serbs called a "reception center." From there the prisoners were sent home. Ari spent seventeen days in Trnopolje before he was released.

Chapter Five

Every morning the prisoners awoke to fear and horror. There seemed to be not even a hint of an end to the savage cruelty—the nightly roll calls, daily interrogations, torture, beatings, screaming, and howling. But what got to the prisoners more than anything else was the complete indifference of their jailers to their misery and pain.

The prisoners were filthy and lice-infested; their wrinkled skin hung loosely from their bodies, barely covering their ribs. The suffering made everyone equal;

they even all began to look alike, as if they'd just been taken out of coffins, hardly moving. An unbearable stench nipped at their nostrils, getting under their skin and leaving a slimy taste in their mouths. The guards only opened the doors every now and then. When they did, the prisoners all turned toward the door to catch a breath of air, to feel like they could still breathe. As the doors shut, they would be beaten. And so it went, for days on end. Prisoners still pushed themselves as close to the door as they could, just to take a single breath of real air, even if they paid for it with a blow to the back from a club or a rifle butt.

For days a man named Muhamed lay by the door; he was thirty-one years old, from Čejrek. He'd had diabetes for several years. His brother, who lived and worked in Germany, had sent him a two-year supply of insulin, figuring things might get bad in Bosnia. Muhamed's younger brother and father were in the same room. They begged the guards in vain to make some kind of arrangement for his medication to be brought to the camp. Muhamed was slowly fading away. His face turned an odd, pale hue. He soon died quietly in his brother's arms. He just stopped breathing.

His eyes stayed wide open, gazing upward. As four men carried Muhamed's lifeless body outside, everyone stood with their heads bent for a long time, expressing their impotence in silence.

Later the prisoners stood the same way as the bodies of Safet Ramadanović, Čamil Pezo, Suljo Ganić (a Croat from Ljubija), Habibović, and others were taken out. They were carried to the lawn in front of the building before being loaded onto a yellow van and taken away. Only the families of Safet Ramadanović, a distinguished restaurant owner from Prijedor, and Suljo Ganić were allowed to come and collect their bodies so they could be properly buried at the city cemetery.

Dying was easy at Omarska, and living was hard. Not even a glimmer of light could be detected at the end of the tunnel. At least in those days, no one found a four-leaf clover in the meadows at the foot of the Kozara Mountains.

The horrendous conditions gave natural selection free reign. Only the strongest and healthiest survived, those who endured the suffering on their own two feet, or those lucky enough not to be called out. Although the math teacher Abdullah Puškar was strong and healthy—built like a boxer, he was almost six feet tall, a hulk of a man—he had the bad luck of having a former student among the guards, a guy who didn't have the fondest memories of school. "Oh, professor, what an honor to find you here with all these hot shots," his old student said cynically the first time he saw Abdullah coming back from the canteen. "I listened to you long enough, now you'll listen to me for a while." He took Abdullah upstairs and, sneering spitefully, ordered him to clean the toilets.

Later, when the former student worked the night shift, he would call Abdullah quite often, leading him out into the night and bringing him back bruised and bloody. Once he just kept beating Abdullah on the head with a club. "I'm gonna beat that math out of you or die trying!" he exclaimed, dumping Abdullah back in the dorm like a sack of potatoes. Abdullah proudly endured the insults and injuries and beatings without complaining, trying to maintain his dignity even under such conditions. His companions in misery nursed his wounds in the hope that the beatings would end one day and he would recover. But late one night his former student called him out once again. Abdullah left a few things behind in the place where he slept. No one ever came for them.

Idriz Jakupović, a well-known public figure in Prijedor, was tortured for days on end. After each interrogation—and there were many—he came back beaten and bloody. Once the guards broke his left arm above the elbow; the end of the broken bone ripped through the muscles of his arm. Another prisoner, Hassan Ališić, tried to adjust the bone, and his efforts seemed to work since Idriz's unbearable pain began to diminish. Hassan made a splint out of a few sticks he found and bandaged the broken arm with a dirty T-shirt. Late one night a guard called Hassan to the door and told him some people from the Omarska "Red Cross" were looking for him. He went out and never came back.

Others not lucky enough to survive the horrors of Omarska included Jasko, who loved motorcycles, and his friend Emir, a policeman, both from Kozarac. They were taken out one evening, stripped, and then beaten with iron rods. Two more prisoners were taken out and, with a knife at their throats, ordered to bite off the genitals of the two young men from Kozarac. As these two died an excruciatingly painful death, the camp resounded with frantic screams.

Equally painful deaths, due to unheard-of abuse and torture, were met by Miro Šolaja, Ilijaz Drobić, Gogi Kardum, Professor Fikret Mujakić-Šicer, Silvo Sarić, Nihad Kadić, and over one thousand other civilian prisoners brought to the Omarska torture chamber from the region of greater Prijedor. "These guys could even give Hitler a run for his money," Dr. Eso Sadiković used to say. "This can't be called Omarska anymore," Djemo would say to himself. "We have to rename it." Each of his words carried the weight of judgment.

Two brothers of Halid Muslimović, the well-known singer from Prijedor, were in the hangar; their names were Senad and Nedžad. Senad was beaten several times. Once, as he was being brought back from interrogation, a guard kept striking his hands with a hammer. Another guard pierced his back with the point of his knife. They forced his feet into two nooses made of electrical cable. Then they hung him by the feet and beat him with truncheons and rods. Senad endured all that and even recovered quite well, although he lost over sixty pounds.

Nedžad was younger, only twenty-three. He was tall and good-looking, with his hair nicely styled. One of the guards scalped him with a knife in the middle of the runway and then made him sing his brother's song, "Bosnia is weeping, weeping. . . ." After the two brothers were transferred to Djemo's dorm, the guards stopped harassing them.

Not all the guards found their nourishment in blood and hatred. A few were good men, honest Serbs. But after a couple of days at Omarska, most such men were sent to the front lines, toward Derventa or Gradačac. That was the last anyone would hear of them. One of them who stayed in the camp the longest was Stole; he was from town, and everyone in Prijedor knew him. He helped his compatriots out as much as he could, even though he knew full well that Serbs who helped Muslims and Croats were punished most severely.

Three Serbs who had been accused of helping "those others" were brought to Omarska: Igor Kondić, his wife Jadranka, and Draško Lujić. Jadranka was let go after two months. After just fifteen days, Draško was transferred to a prison in Banja Luka before going to trial. Igor, whose father happened to have been born in the town of Omarska, underwent horrible torture for a few days before the guards killed him.

The best of all the guards was Željko, also known as Džigi; he was forty years old and a partner in a gas station at Omarska. He never once hit anybody. His post was under the window of Djemo's dorm. He often threw a piece of bread or a freshly picked plum through the window. Djemo knew him from before; they had even been friends. On his first day as a guard at Omarska, Džigi had called to Djemo and said openly, in front of all the prisoners, "Djemo, you're the prisoner and I'm the guard, but you were my friend before, and that's how you'll stay." As he said it, he gave Djemo a firm handshake. "I'll do whatever I can, just don't expect any miracles." Djemo thought he saw a tear roll down Džigi's unshaven face. Later Džigi brought food from home and secretly passed it on to Djemo. Sometimes he took Djemo to the canteen and let him eat a lot more than his ration. He even brought messages from home, from Alma and Deni. He was the first to let Djemo know that his son had been released from the camp at Trnopolje.

Once he knocked on the window frame over

Djemo's head with the tip of his rifle and, speaking softly so the other guards wouldn't hear, told Djemo to put his head out through the broken window because he wanted to tell him something. The window was rather high, just below the ceiling, so Djemo put one foot on the radiator, held on to the window frame with his healthy hand, and stuck his head out through the broken glass. "I'll call you again in about fifteen minutes. I've got something for you," Džigi said, winking at him. Soon enough, he knocked on the window again and handed Djemo a big plastic bowl covered with a lid. "Here, share this with your friends, and then give me back the bowl." The bowl was filled with macaroni and meat in a thick broth. Džigi told Djemo later that the food was meant for the guards, but since it was a Serbian holiday all the guards, according to custom, were having roast meat and plum brandy. So their dinner went to warm up some of the shrunken stomachs of those on the inside.

"Make sure you give some of this food to Balada," Džigi used to say whenever he had something extra for Djemo. Balada was a young man from Djemo's neighborhood; he lived in the third house down on the left from Djemo's building. He was a great guy, always there when his friends needed him. One afternoon the guards called Balada, Hućo, Emir, and Šabo and took them over toward the White House. The next day someone from the other dorm told Djemo: "I loaded Balada's body onto the yellow van today." When Djemo told Džigi what had happened, the news really got to him. The next day, as soon as Džigi came on duty, he called Djemo over and said, "Watch yourself, Djemo, all right? I'll tell you straight out, the first thing I do whenever I come in is to look at the lists. If I ever see your name, they'll have to get by me first."

As it happened, Džigi was in the most notorious group of guards; it was called "Krkan's shift," after its potbellied leader. It was also known as "the terror shift." The worst of the group were Paspalj and Šoške, as they were called by the other guards. They killed people for the hell of it, without the least pretext. If they didn't like a prisoner's face or the way he moved, it was all over. They once gave Bajram Zgog, who used to coach and play for the famous Rudar soccer club, ten minutes to collect two hundred German marks from the other prisoners. (Even they themselves put no trust in the money printed up by their self-appointed "Serb Republic.") Ten minutes later they came back and told him to give them the money.

"I don't have it," Zgog said. He hadn't even tried to get it, knowing that the poor wretches in his dorm couldn't possibly have still held on to that kind of money. The prisoners standing near him were ordered to move back. Šoške stayed near the door, with his rifle cocked and his finger on the trigger. Paspalj came up to Zgog and began beating him so viciously that everyone watching felt like their hearts were being ripped apart. Suddenly Zgog leaped over the crumpled-up bodies of the dazed prisoners. He got to the window and, raising his hands high over his head, took a swing at it. Shattered glass fell all over the place. He grabbed a piece of glass and tried to slash his wrists with it, preferring to put an end to himself rather than fall into the hands of the brutes. A few prisoners jumped him to stop him from going through with it. After that, Paspalj and Šoške took him out. None of the prisoners ever saw Zgog again.

Another time, in the heat of passionate hatred, one of the guards went up to Braco Burazerović as he sat with some other prisoners on the runway after a meal.

Braco used to work for the Yugoslav army in that district. The guard asked, "You the same Braco that used to do recruiting for the army?" "Yes, that's me, Braco," he answered, his voice betraying a strange foreboding. "You motherfucker! When I was there, you didn't want to send me into the armored division. So, Braco, now it's time to meet your maker!" And Braco was led off in the direction of the White House.

When new prisoners were brought to the camp—and there were new arrivals almost every day—they were given a bloody welcome with all kinds of truncheons as soon as they stepped out of the bus. Many never made it as far as the dorm: the guards would have smashed their heads against the brick wall of the building. That was truly a horrible sound—a skull being smashed, the bones splitting and breaking. That sound, intermingled with shouts and painful screams, penetrated deep into the guts of the people inside, scorching their very eardrums. It circled and hovered, like a flock of black ravens, high over the entire region of Kozara. This bloody reality, like a frozen apparition, became sealed upon their very souls. Fear got under their skin, penetrating deep into their bones, traversing their veins, then breaking out all over their bodies in tiny beads of sweat. It was as if evil had been buried in every clump of this border land.

All may be fair in love and war, but practices such as those at Omarska were the most perverse forms of physical and psychological torture—a militarily enforced prostitution of people, supplied by a huge arsenal of pain and suffering. Mujica, a well-known musician from Prijedor and a real card, spoke a bitter truth: every morning when he got up, as he touched his face and body with his fingers, he'd say, "It's okay, I woke up alive again!" Two or three months after he finally got out of the camp, Mujica died in Prijedor in his own house. His kidneys gave out. He couldn't get the medicine he needed, and he couldn't get out of Prijedor. He had just turned thirty.

"Their souls are steeped in atrocities and hatred, so they feed on our blood and our bodies," people said. "But they can't possibly annihilate all of us." The picture of a man made to drink dirty motor oil is unforgettable. Or a guard firing into the back of a defenseless man's head and forcing every witness to applaud. The fear petrified upon the scorched face of Durat, who used to be a goalie on the Prijedor soccer team, as the guards pushed his head through a burning tire. A scrawny, dried-up skeleton of a man tearing apart a dead pigeon for food. A son weeping as he is forced to watch the bloodthirsty monsters plunge daggers into his father's body.

Their suffering found a place to reside between sunset and sunrise. The stench of dead and decaying bodies. No, none of this could ever be forgotten. Djemo remembered a poem by the Bosnian poet Izet Sarajlić:

There were twenty-eight
There were five thousand twenty-eight
More than there'd ever been
In a single poem there were lovers
Who'd now be fathers
But they're gone now
Now in Lover's Lane
They await the grave
Oh my little one
My great love
Tonight let's love each
Other in their name

Chapter Six

The Omarska camp wasn't surrounded by barbed wire, but it was as secure as a stone fortress. It was encircled by three rings of guards, with thirty guards in each ring. One ring was in the camp, the second some fifty yards beyond, and the third about one hundred yards from the first ring. The first and second group kept an eye on the camp itself, to make sure no prisoners tried to run away; the third protected the camp from any possible invaders.

Only two prisoners managed to get through all three

rings and escape. The first was captured by residents of the nearby Serbian village, Gradina, and brought back. He was killed immediately. The second got about six miles from Omarska, making it to the ruins of his village, Kozaruša; he hid out there in the rubble for a month or so. When he relaxed a bit, he set off for Prijedor. There he was shot in the leg and captured. Later he was brought back to the Omarska camp. No one knows what happened to him after that. Some say he died of infections, since his wounds were never treated.

Such deaths, of course, were commonplace, especially from wounds inflicted by sharp, rusty objects. After a day or two of bleeding, the area around the wound would swell and turn purple. Then a scab would form as pus continued to run from the wound. One prisoner even took worms out of his own head wound, the kind that normally appear on corpses when they start to rot. By some miracle, he survived.

Some prisoners prevailed over their fear of death only by maintaining the meager and desperate hope that all the misery would have to come to an end sometime. Malnourished and weak, suffering from scurvy, with legs like sticks, the prisoners moved like the living dead. Greasy collars and rags full of lice hung off their skeletons. Sweaty and barefoot, their sunken cheeks the color of wax, they looked more and more like ghosts. The unbearable heat, the flies swarming everywhere, the lice in their hair and clothes—all these conditions bore little resemblance to life as they had known it. For those whose acceptance of their fate was absolute, even their last glimmer of hope was dimmed. Hopelessness and apathy warmed their bodies as the sense of humiliation grew day by day. And time—that final arbiter of mortality—moved along slowly, very slowly.

It was a time of crying without tears, without noise. Even prayers couldn't be heard. It was as if the prisoners had been both tried and sentenced to endure the evil of the camp. Everything around them turned to sadness. Even the oldest among them couldn't remember a sadder summer. The grass was burned by the sun hanging high over Mount Kozara. At night only a sliver of the moon crept across the sky. Drop by drop, death continued to trickle over the bare chests of the helpless souls inside. Death was carried in the eyes of their jailers, whose very bodies had become weapons, whose every step rang like a death rattle. Several thousand lives were held in the balance between life and death by the fingers on the triggers, by the hands on the daggers, by the bits of paper stuffed into the small pockets of the bloody uniforms the guards discarded like used tissues. This was the fate of people from Čarakovo, Bišćani, Rizvanović, Kevljan, Ljubija, Šurkovac, Kozarac . . . from the burned-out villages near Prijedor.

Most of the victims who came through Omarska were from Kozarac; their homes had also been hit the hardest. The residents of Kozarac were either killed on the spot or driven out in the long columns of pain flowing from the points of the daggers held by former neighbors. They were marched into the camps around Prijedor: Brezičani, Keraterm, Trnopolje, Omarska. Among the two thousand people from Kozara crammed into Omarska were Kasim Grozdanić, a fifty-five-year-old shopkeeper, and his son Suad, nicknamed "Sudo" by his friends. They spent their days as prisoners in the hangar, the building across the runway from Djemo's dorm. They were captured when they and some of their neighbors had attempted, through the hail of artillery shells that destroyed their village, to get to Mount Kozara and then across the mountains, under the protection of the forest. Wanting only to get as far as possible from the hell that had enveloped them, they didn't even know where they were heading. They were captured along with hundreds of others and taken to the police station in Prijedor. After being tortured for two days, they were transferred to Omarska. Kasim's brother and his three sons were with them.

First they were placed in "Twenty-Six," the notorious dorm above the hangar, and then down below in the hangar's huge hall where more than one thousand prisoners spent their days. The bare cement, covered with puddles of gasoline and dirty motor oil, was all they had to sleep on. The space they slept in was surrounded by a ring of barbed wire. There were smaller dorms upstairs, where between forty-five and fifty prisoners were kept. In the highest part of the hangar, about forty-five feet above the floor, pigeons nestled in between the asbestos room and the huge steel girders. At every flap of their wings, lice plummeted off their feathers onto the poor wretches below. The unbearable stench made everyone nauseous. There were no windows that opened anywhere, only tiny glass brick skylights at the peak of the roof. Occasionally the guards opened the big doors through which broken equipment had been ferried in and out in the old days.

Kasim and Sudo were right by the steps in the hangar that led to the small dorms, the former offices of the mine administrators. Kasim had taken off his old windbreaker and put it down for his son to lie on. Sudo just lay on the bare and dirty cement. Anxiety was deeply etched into Kasim's sunken cheeks. White shocks, premature signs of old age, ran through his hair. His face had a yellowish pallor, but his eyes still expressed an odd sense of defiance.

Sudo was just twenty-four. The spark of manhood was in his eyes, since he had left youth behind. Tall and well built, he had been the kind of guy any girl would fall head over heels for, but he was fading away now, from day to day. His youthful face had taken on a stony color as his eyes began to sink and lose their shine, the dark circles growing beneath them. His skin had begun to sag and wrinkle. His skinny legs stuck out, as if planted in the cement. Like so many others, he had contracted dysentery from the bad food and filthy conditions. Could there be any misery worse than this, rushing for the toilet every second, as your bleeding guts try to force themselves out? Often such a prisoner couldn't make it and lost control, the excrement running down the legs of his pants as it soiled the bodies huddled along the floor on the way to the toilet. There was always a guard in the hangar next to the toilet, ready to administer a beating.

Sudo got so weak he couldn't even go and eat. So his father didn't go either. Kasim didn't want to leave his son alone for even a minute. With some German marks he had managed to hide, Kasim bought some biscuits to feed Sudo. "You have to eat, son, it'll make you feel better. You have to get better," Kasim would say, as if he were uttering some magical incantation. Sudo would prop himself up, leaning on one arm, just enough to let his father put the cookie in his mouth. Then he'd chew for a long time until, a painful grimace on his face, he forced it down, choking on a coughing fit brought on by his stomach cramps.

The overwhelming heat pinched at Kasim's eyes, and he often felt the need to cry, to just scream out loud with all his strength. It seemed to him that doing so would have made things easier, but he didn't do it, because of his son. His misery was gathered into the few glistening drops that slid slowly down his parched cheeks. But his eyes retained the fury of curses as he cracked his knuckles and raised his head upward, toward the sky, to pray to God.

"Out, everybody out," barked one of the guards as he came in and stood with his back to the huge doors. Kasim knew that Sudo would have to go out too; he didn't dare ask whether his son could stay. And even if the guard had said he could, there was no way Kasim could trust him. Kasim helped his son up onto his weak legs and managed to get him outside in front of the hangar.

"Take off all your clothes, everything," one of the guards shouted angrily. "We can't even go into the hangar because of your stink." Another guard held a thick rubber hose that blasted a stream of water onto the asphalt surface. Kasim felt unspeakable shame that his son had to see and endure such humiliation. The skinny bodies looked even more pathetic without the rags covering them. They were taken out ten at a time to be hosed down. Kasim and Sudo's turn came. When they were just a few yards from the guard with the hose, he began to douse them. The powerful stream of cold water beat down on them like truncheons. Laughing and joking, the guards kept up the merciless game between the water and the paltry, weakened bodies for a long time.

Sudo twisted, turning his back to the water. Biting his lower lip from pain, he tried to protect himself with his hands as he avoided looking at his father. Kasim tried to use his own body to shield his son from the powerful impact of the water. Some men screamed as the water pounded on their open wounds. The healthier ones tried to catch a few drops of water in their mouths to moisten their parched throats, but the pressure of the water almost choked them. The guards just kept pointing at them and laughing cynically. They thoroughly enjoyed the spectacle of helplessness. Even though it didn't last long, it seemed to go on forever. Afterward the prisoners pulled on the tattered remains of their clothes and ran back to their spots in the hangar. Kasim and Sudo were among the last to return.

As they entered the hangar, the guards clubbed them on their backs and heads with truncheons, cursing all the while. Kasim's shirt got caught on the door handle. Before he knew it, at least ten truncheons were pummeling his back. He tugged at the shirt until it tore, freeing him to run into the fenced-off area in the hangar and escape an even fiercer beating.

That night Sudo ran a fever and the pains in his stomach got worse. An awful and treacherous boom rang through his head. He barely recognized the voices of the men around him. Dimly, he saw his father's anxious face and felt Kasim's fingers stroking his hair, soaked in sweat. The light in the bulb shining through the broken fixture outside created patterns across his face. "Dad, I . . . ," Sudo whispered, barely audible, as his father inched closer to hear what his son was saying. "I don't regret dying, Dad, as long as I can stop looking at this. What did we ever do to them anyway?" Kasim looked away so that his son wouldn't see the tears in his eyes.

From the tiny skylights above, the first light of day began to appear. Sudo's breathing became more difficult, then softer and shorter. Life slowly ebbed from his withered body. Little by little, the light of his twenty-four years extinguished itself. "Please, Dad . . . ," and his last words withered on his lips. A heavy, dead silence reigned throughout the hangar. Off in a corner, someone cursed God.

Kasim got up, straightened himself, and stood still for a long time, as if he had turned to stone. His tears dried. His face twisted, contorted by the hatred rising within him. He bit his fist to staunch the sobbing that, like a flood, felt as if it would drown him. He looked but could see and hear nothing. He didn't weep with his eyes but with his soul, with a father's pain. With the death of his son, lying here beside him, he had lost his main reason for living. The image of his dead son burned itself into his heart and would smolder there, like a glowing ember. How would he tell his wife, if she was still alive, that their son—her darling boy, the apple of her eye—was gone? And what about Suada, Sudo's dear sister?

Kasim just stood there as a guard came up to him. "What's the matter with this one over here?" he asked, kicking the lifeless body. Kasim didn't say a word, but his eyes passed over the guard like a dagger. His look, full of hatred and contempt, was almost like a stab in the face. "This one's been dead at least three days by now. Get this garbage out of here," the guard said, not bothering to hide his barbaric cruelty. Kasim's mouth began to move, to say something or spit in the guard's face, but his numbed lips couldn't budge. He stood there like a deaf mute, looking at Sudo's dead body as if he were pledging an oath to some invisible form of justice that he would one day fulfill in his son's name.

Kasim kept standing like that when his brother and his brother's sons carried the dead body out and took it over by the White House. They left Sudo's body on the grass where a few other corpses were piled. Later all the corpses were loaded onto the yellow truck. "His youth will be buried somewhere in these trenches," Kasim said quietly. "Will I ever find out where?" He would live the rest of his life settling accounts.

Chapter Seven

The day after Sudo's death, early in the morning on August 6, the roll call went on longer than it ever had before. Kasim was among those whose name was called out. With their rags under their arms, the prisoners went out onto the runway. They lined up in rows of ten, waiting to see what would happen next. A guard with a mustache called the names; other guards brought more lists every now and then with the names of more prisoners. Everyone was confused. Never had so many names been called, and in broad daylight to boot. "They can't just take all of us and . . . ," Djemo didn't even dare let his suspicion reach its logical conclusion.

One group was taken aside; Djemo's cousins Fadil and Fudo were in it. And then the news broke: they were heading home. All the misery would be coming to an end. "Omarska is closing down!" The word spread in a whisper from mouth to mouth. Names were called out until late afternoon, when the first bus arrived, from the town of Omarska, wrapped in a cloud of dust, followed by a second and a third. More than twenty buses pulled in. Faint smiles began to quiver on the prisoners' faces, so long unaccustomed to expressing such a curious sense of well-being. Embracing one another, they shed tears of joy. Even Djemo felt something like a smile, though it appeared more like a grimace: "Can this really be the end?"

The prisoners made no attempt to hide their happiness from the guards, but the cynical sneers they were met with did not bode well. The buses lined up nearby. Along with the buses were two army trucks and about ten well-armed soldiers. The prisoners who had been housed in the garage for the last few days got into the first two buses. The rest were organized into groups. Muharem Nezirević, formerly a producer at Radio Prijedor, was in Djemo's group, along with Sead Softić, an optician from Kozarac who used to have a shop in Prijedor. Halid Muslimović's brothers, Senad and Nedžad, were in the second bus.

Djemo didn't know anyone else. As soon as they got on the bus they were ordered to bow their heads. Over one hundred people were stuffed onto and under the seats, on the floor, and on top of each other in a bus that normally seated forty. Djemo invited two younger men he didn't know to share his seat, the second on the right behind the driver. Muharem and Sead sat across from them. After about half an hour three soldiers climbed onto each bus and they set out. Some buses headed toward the camp at Trnopolje, from where the prisoners would later be released. But all the other buses, carrying around thirteen hundred prisoners, headed in the opposite direction, toward the notorious camp at Manjača. One hundred eighty-four prisoners remained at Omarska.

The convoy of buses was accompanied on either side by the "boys" from Prijedor's Special Intervention

Forces; they rode in army trucks, their machine guns pointed and ready. The commander-in-chief of that gang of punks was Zoran Babić; nicknamed "Bakin," he had been quite an athlete and was even considered one of Prijedor's great hopefuls. Now his athletic feats amounted to carrying a Scorpion in his right hand, always uncocked at elbow level.

The buses stopped at the entrance to the village of Omarska. Every prisoner with a serious or visible wound was ordered off the bus. No one volunteered, since they knew this meant a slit throat or, as the Serbs liked to call it, "the shortcut." Then a guy named Mrdja came barreling onto the bus with a club and began beating everyone; he just stepped on the prisoners lying on the floor between the rows of seats as he flailed away. Djemo got hit twice on the head and once on the side, in his ribs. He again felt that unutterable pain, but he neither moved nor cried out. Such responses only further excited the wild beasts. As the trip continued, Mrdja and his "interventionists" often stopped the bus to "intervene."

The buses were old and run-down. Before, they had been used only for short routes through town on well-paved streets; now they could barely move their loads. The drivers wore uniforms with Serb insignias. While the heat outside made it seem like the sky had been set on fire, it was even worse inside. The drivers periodically turned the heat on, bringing the temperature up to the boiling point. The sweat flowing off the prisoners soaked their torn bits of clothing and ran down their scrawny bodies, creating the asphyxiating smell of dead air. Their trials were far from over.

And so they got to Banja Luka, the largest and loveliest city in the region. "Everything that's happening to us is our fault," thought Djemo, as they drove through the outskirts of town, along the service road that led to Jajce. Banja Luka was once much smaller and quainter; the Turkish word *sheher*, an archaic word for "downtown," truly conveyed the atmosphere of its picturesque Old City, the old Muslim part of town. After the earthquake in 1969, everyone pitched in to help restore the "Crown Jewel" of the border lands between the Austro-Hungarian and the Ottoman empires. No one regretted either the expense or the work involved. Djemo himself had been part of a volunteer youth corps that helped rebuild the ruins. New apartment buildings, schools, and nurseries were built. A modern bustling city arose from the ashes, full of wide avenues and parks. "Now it really has become the Crown Jewel," people said. After the earthquake many newcomers came to settle in Banja Luka, not only from every part of Bosnia but from other republics as well. They brought their attitudes and customs with them, building a city from both their virtues and their short-comings.

Now it was a cold city, the seat of the so-called Serbian Region of Krajina, the very place from which the infectious germ of discord had begun to spread. Thousands of armed warriors strolled around the city, ready to kill in the name of that pipe dream of a state, ready to drive out neighbors and friends, people who had only recently been best man at their weddings or godfather to their children. Such Serbs were even ready to drive out their own relatives—brothers- and sisters-in-law—to expel them from land and homes inhabited by their families for centuries, not recognizing the utter mindlessness and folly of such politics. Because of them, this old border land had become swollen with corpses.

"Who knows, maybe if it hadn't been for the earthquake . . . ," Djemo thought to himself.

When the buses passed through the Old City, one of the guards asked the driver to open the front door. The driver pressed a button, and with a hissing noise, the door opened. Then the guard took out his machine gun, stuck the barrel out the door, and fired a long round at the minaret of the mosque the bus had been about to pass. His cohorts gleefully congratulated him for the gesture. "Sooner or later the day of reckoning for all this will come," Djemo said to himself, as the sweat on his face made him squint until he buried his head still further into his folded hands. They turned off the main road toward the hills, along a smaller, narrow, but still paved road. Before long the asphalt gave way to cobblestone, and then to dirt, overgrown by the surrounding woods.

After a few miles the buses stopped again. The "boys" from the army trucks, with looks of absolute contempt, leaped out armed with wooden sticks and spread through all the buses. In a frenzy they beat everyone, stepping all over the prisoners and kicking them with their boots. They asked who came from Kozarac. No one said a word. Then Mrdja the wildman, with his long unkempt hair, went from one man to the next, grabbing each man by the hair and drawing his face close to look him fiercely in the eyes.

"Well, look who's here, even you, little birdy!" he said, holding Dado, the owner of the Amadeus Café in Prijedor, by the hair and leading him to the door of the bus. He threw him out with such force that Dado ended up sprawled across the full length of the dusty road. Mrdja drew a pistol out of his holster and pushed Dado in front of him, pointing toward the nearest patch of woods. When they got past some trees, he ordered Dado to stop and kneel down. Dado obeyed silently, making peace with his fate, but there was fear in his eyes, the fear of a man facing execution. Mrdja brought the pistol up to Dado's head, but just as his index finger started to flex, a shout rang out: "Mrdjaaaa, not him, please!"

Mrdja was startled and turned toward the voice calling to him. One of his "interventionists" ran up: "Not him, he's a friend of mine." Mrdja flashed a wicked smile, showing his rotten teeth, covered with tobacco stains. "He's a good one, I give you my word, I know him, I used to be a waiter in his café," the soldier said, helping Dado get up off the ground. "You can have him then," said Mrdja. "Take him, who cares if he fucks you over, but just remember: the only good Muslim is a dead Muslim!"

Mrdja put his pistol back in the holster, turned around, and climbed into one of the army trucks, leaving Dado and his former waiter standing there. As the two returned to the buses, Mrdja called to Dado: "Come kiss this," pointing to a little plastic crocodile hanging off one of the machine-gun barrels in the truck. Dado came up and kissed the plastic crocodile. The occupants of the truck broke out cackling like lunatics. "He saved your life, now get your ass back into that bus before I change my mind," Mrdja shouted.

Then the sad column picked up and continued on its journey of terror. At the end of the dirt road the buses were stopped by a large group of soldiers from the boot camp next to the road. "*Ustasha* motherfuckers, let us at 'em!" one of the soldiers exclaimed. "Ever notice how much they stink," another added, peering into the bus for a second. One soldier wedged his rifle through the rear doors of the bus, trying to see what he could stick with the bayonet on the end. Luckily he didn't stab anyone. The frightened men simply kept quiet, enduring whatever came next.

A raunchy-looking soldier came off the truck and into the bus. "Anybody by the name of Nezir Krak in here?" He was looking for an auto mechanic who had owned his own shop in Prijedor. Everyone, including Nezir—on the floor in the back of the bus—kept quiet; besides suffering from the heat, he was also enduring the pain of broken ribs, the result of a beating a few days earlier at Omarska. The soldier left, then came back in a few minutes. "I'm looking for Nezir Krak, and I know he's on this bus." Again no answer; the only sound was the rhythmic chugging of the engine. "What kind of an asshole do you take me for? Is everyone deaf? Hello, anyone out there hear me? Nezir Krak has ten seconds to give himself up, otherwise I'm going to unload a round right here." As the lout issued his threat, the sound of another round being fired somewhere else could be heard. "Here I am," Nezir called out, unwilling to let this bloodthirsty creature carry out his threat.

"Get out, motherfucker! You *Ustasha* bastard! And your father was *Ustasha* too. The seed never falls far from the tree."

"I can't get up, I'm sick. I can't get onto my feet," Nezir said.

"You listen to me, you miserable piece of Muslim shit, get out before I start right here . . . ," and the soldier trailed off without completely finishing his threat, moving toward the back of the bus as he kicked everyone along the way. Nezir barely managed to drag himself out from under a pile of bodies, whose owners, overcome by fear, didn't let out so much as the sound of their breathing. He moved toward the open door of the bus; outside another three or four "boys" from the army truck stood waiting, including Mrdja and Bakin. They stripped Nezir naked and beat him, cursing his *Ustasha* mother. They cut him with their knives and drew the letter *U* on his forehead. Finally, one of them pierced him through from below with a real, honest-to-God sword. Nezir's tortured body simply trembled, for just a few seconds, before dropping in a horrible death rattle. The soldiers opened up the luggage compartment under the bus and tossed his body in like a sack of potatoes. Then, as if nothing had happened, they jumped back into their truck and headed on.

It was only a few miles from there to the entrance of

the Manjača camp. It was already dark by the time the buses arrived at the gate, whose huge letters greeted them: MANAČA MILITARY CAMP NO ENTRANCE. The trip from Omarska to Manjača had lasted more than six hours, even though they had gone only about thirty-five miles. The drivers lined up next to each other in a narrow lane in front of the gate. Word spread that the prisoners would spend the night in the buses since they couldn't be processed after dark: there was no electricity at the camp. None of them had even begun to imagine the night of horrors awaiting them.

First, all the windows were shut tight and the heat turned up full blast. The men were hungry, thirsty, and exhausted but didn't even dare move from their contorted positions. Some—with great stealth, so the soldiers wouldn't see or hear them—wrang out bits of their tattered clothing and used the sweat to moisten their blistered lips. Later the driver came on, turned off the engine and the heater, and left. The escorts also left.

The eerie silence lasted around ten minutes. "You got a Dedo Crnalić on this bus?" came the first call in the bus right next to Djemo. Now they were after Dedo, a guy everyone in Prijedor knew, the owner of one of the nicest restaurants in town, an athlete, and someone always involved in one public office or another. As he was getting out, one of the beasts said, "Now let me show you how hamburger meat should be ground up," and drew a sharp knife across Dedo's back, right at the door of the bus. Blood splattered all over everyone crumpled up on top of each other by the door. They could hear Dedo's blood gurgling and his breath expiring as his body went into convulsions; then the deathly silence returned.

It lasted only a minute or two before the soldiers called for three prisoners to put Dedo's corpse back on the bus. No one volunteered. One of the soldiers climbed on the bus and threw out the first three men nearest the door. With their jaws frozen in fear, they brought the bloody, lifeless body in and put it on one of the seats, following orders. From outside came the cackles and screeches of wild animals aroused by the smell of fresh blood. A brutal lust permeated the eyes of the killing machines. God Almighty, when would the nightmare come to an end?

Djemo stayed huddled over, his head against his arms crossed in front of him, leaning on the steel bar above the seat in front. There was no one sitting in that front seat. No one dared sit so close to the escorts. Between the back of the seat and the metal bar was an opening a fraction of an inch wide through which Djemo could see the front of the bus. He saw a soldier get on holding a rough-cut wooden club, the length and thickness of an arm. The last thing he saw was the guy stepping forward and lifting the club. He felt a sharp pain in his head. "That's it for you, Djemo. You're history, kiddo." He recognized Mrdja's voice as the blows rained down on his head and back. With his left hand, he tried to fend them off and cover his head. Mrdja lowered the club, pulled out a pistol, and put it to Djemo's forehead. "You put your hand like that just one more time, and I'll kill you like a dog." Then he hit Djemo again even harder than before. Djemo felt the kind of pain that knocks the sense out of a man. Blood was all over his hair, face, and neck, flooding his filthy, sweat-soaked T-shirt. Djemo raised his head. Looking straight into the eyes that had signaled his bloody end, he said: "Look what you're doing to me! What have I ever done to you?"

His question took Mrdja by surprise. Glancing away

from Djemo's blood-covered face, to his right, Mrdja saw Muharem Nezirević, the Radio Prijedor producer. "Ah, my little birdy, you again!" He started clubbing Muharem on the head. "So you didn't want to put any news of the war from the front on, right?" "I did, I did put it on," Muharem said, trying to sink even further under the seat, to save himself from the mighty blows. "Yeah, I know, you did it because you had to, but you didn't put enough on. Now you'll see what Serb soldiers are made of. Move your ass!" Mrdja shouted.

Muharem got up and stepped out of the bus, covering his face and head with his hands and arms, but he got a boot to the stomach and a fist hammered into the top of his head. "Enough," came a commanding voice from the front of the bus. "That's the kind of thing you were supposed to do in Omarska, but you can't do it here." Later the prisoners learned that the voice belonged to the commander-in-chief and supervising officer of Manjača. Muharem got back onto the bus quickly, taking advantage of the momentary confusion. A thin stream of blood flowed down his face from a cut on his forehead. Then the driver came on board, turned off the lights in the bus, closed the door, and went out.

Peace and darkness took over. The men didn't even dare breathe too loudly. They trembled, as if it were the middle of winter. The stale, humid air made everyone nauseous. Thirst withered their shriveled lips. Every now and then one of the braver ones rose from the bodies piled in heaps to run his fingers across the damp glass of the window and wet his lips with the tiny drops. The worst part of the dryness settled in their throats. No one even thought about sleep. The blood on Djemo's face, neck, and hair was drying. He pecked with his fingers at the cakelike mass that covered his face like a mask. The dried blood crumbled into fine dust between his fingers and fell into his lap. He could feel a swelling in his head and hand.

Around five in the morning they were taken out into a field near the buses. Two prisoners didn't get out of Djemo's bus; they were already dead. Some new soldiers joined the escorts. The prisoners were called out by name and led through the gates of the camp in groups of one hundred. Among those who didn't make it were Djuzin, Bašić, Jama, and a young man known as Munja. The journey of terror from Omarska to Manjača had cost nine men their lives.

Chapter Eight

The first order of business in the Manjača camp was a medical exam. On Djemo's file they wrote: "Right arm broken; one broken rib; fractured skull with internal hemorrhaging in several areas. Medical care required." The medical exams lasted all day. The prisoners hadn't eaten for two days but were given only water. In the evening they were taken to the dorms. These were actually empty stalls for livestock, with cement floors covered in ferns to use for beds.

"This is where you'll stay," announced the man in charge. "You are now in Manjača, and I am the supervisor of this camp. You must follow some elementary rules that apply around here. This is one of them: head down and hands behind your back. You must respect work, order, and discipline. If you do that, no one will hurt you. This I personally promise to you."

Later the prisoners learned that the supervisor was known as Špaga, and that he was a good man who protected prisoners. They heard about him from people who had already been in the camp for months. There were prisoners at Manjača from Sanski Most, Ključ, Doboj, Bosanska Dubica, Glamoč, Prijedor, and many other places. All in all, there were about four thousand prisoners divided into six stalls; Špaga referred to them as pavilions. One unit comprised three stalls, along with the covered area where the field mess was located. The unit was surrounded by two barbed-wire fences, with a minefield in between. A wooden sign that said "MINES" in Cyrillic script hung off the barbed wire. There were guards everywhere, with machine guns and dogs, standing in front of guardhouses. Because of their camouflage uniforms, the prisoners called them "pied pipers."

Prisoners couldn't go from one unit to another without a special permit, which wasn't easy to get. The prisoners worked in the kitchen. They were given two meals a day: breakfast at around six o'clock in the morning and lunch at three in the afternoon. For the first few days the food wasn't much better than at Omarska.

Later there were visits by representatives of the International Red Cross, and the prisoners began to receive supplies. The food got better and better each day. The prisoners lived from one meal to the next, eating in silence. Their bodies were heavy with pain when they emerged from their stalls like shadows and went off to eat. Their steps were uncertain. Some fell from weakness as they waited in line for lunch. They would simply collapse into the dust, gathering at the feet of the others still standing, who would eat their rations. Water would be poured over them, and then, as if nothing had happened, they would go back to their food and hungrily empty their plates. Often they licked them clean, wanting to consume every last crumb and force more food into their gaping stomachs.

One day Vojo Kuprešanin, one of the founding fathers of the whole tragedy they were now living through, came to visit. He said that they would soon be going home, and that Serbs, Muslims, and Croats had to live together since Bosnia-Herzegovina was home to them all. He went on and on. The men applauded, hoping against hope.

Such meager hopes kept them going. Only thirty at a time were allowed to leave a stall to spend half an hour on the grass. The soldier in charge of Djemo's stall was Sakib Bešić; everyone called him the Lieutenant Colonel. His assistants were Šemso Halilagić and Feho Fazlić. It was they who maintained calm and order in the stall.

The men were aching from their wounds. But the wounds on their souls were even deeper and more painful than those on their bodies. Worry and hurt were etched into their eyes. When evening enveloped the camp, an even greater sadness arrived. The nights were very cold on that strange mountainside, and often rainy. Thunder and lightning would rip the sky apart. Bolts of lightning lit up a whole stall. The unexpected flash clearly revealed the curled-up bodies on the heaps of fern for just an instant. As morning came, the rain-bearing clouds would disperse.

The cooks got up early, around three in the morning, to prepare breakfast. The guards woke everyone else up at 5:00 A.M.; the prisoners could wash then, if there was any water. After washing they lined up in their stalls, heads down, hands behind their backs, and went to breakfast in pairs.

The biggest problem at Manjača was water. Drinking water was brought by the soldiers in trucks from a well a few miles away and poured into large plastic canisters on wooden tables in front of each stall. After filling a smaller canister with water, one prisoner would raise it by its straps while another prisoner poured water from it into a small plastic cup; so they went, down the line, filling and refilling the cup as each prisoner took a drink.

Later the Red Cross distributed plastic water bottles so that each prisoner—again in line—could get his own refill from the big barrel. After that the commanding officers claimed that a shortage of diesel fuel prevented them from continuing to bring well water in, so the soldiers would take two hundred men at a time from each stall and lead them to the nearest lake, which also served for underwater training with amphibious tanks.

The water was dirty, thick with greenish weeds and branches. Once a guard took a group to the lake and, after pissing in the lake in front of the prisoners, ordered them to fill their bottles. That water was also used in the kitchen. When the Red Cross visitors took a sample from the lake, they said the water wasn't even fit for livestock. The camp administrators were given diesel fuel so they could once again bring well water in. But the trucks transported water from the wells only two more times. Then the prisoners had to go back to making two trips a day to the lake with their water bottles.

When it rained, the prisoners put their plastic bowls under the rain gutters to catch water they could drink. They also washed in the rain, since showers had been organized only once by the camp officials. Once over the course of one hundred days, groups of twenty prisoners were given two minutes to get their bodies wet.

International Red Cross representatives brought white powder and shampoo that helped get rid of the lice infesting every single prisoner. They came every Wednesday, and occasionally more often. The first time they came they wrote down the names of all the prisoners and everyone got a card with his first and last name and a registration number. The prisoners were told that they were now registered in the main computer database in Geneva and that the Red Cross would keep track of each prisoner's whereabouts. Djemo's number was 00207817.

Every other Wednesday each prisoner got a pack of cigarettes; these were, of course, Manjača's most cherished commodity. For two cigarettes a prisoner could buy an extra lunch; ten would buy a shirt. Shoes, also from the Red Cross, cost a bit more. A good pair went for several packs. Nothing went to waste; the prisoners even cut playing cards out of the shoe boxes. Nedžad Muslimović made the best ones. Usually they played old maid or gin rummy. The real card sharks played for cigarettes.

From the heavier cardboard of cigarette cartons they made chess boards. They drew figures on squares of cardboard and arranged them on the board. Both chess and cards were played only when the pied pipers weren't expected in the stall. The best chess player was Refik Šišić, a great hairdresser from Prijedor. (There had been a false rumor that he was killed in the first raids against the city.) One prisoner even carved chess pieces out of wood. He pinched a spoon from the canteen and, after breaking it, filed the handle down against the cement until the edge was nice and sharp. That became his carving tool. Others followed suit and made cigarette holders, tiny airplanes, and small figures of men, head down and hands behind the back.

Fifteen days after Djemo's group arrived, the 184 prisoners who had been left behind in Omarska were transferred to Manjača.

The food got better and better. Sometimes they even got fruit, an apple or a tangerine. The rough, sagging skin on their faces started to tighten and regain its shine. A sparkle came back to their eyes. Once in a while a smile even forced its way across a prisoner's face.

The days, surrounded by barbed wire and mines, went by very slowly. Life had slowed down to a deadly pace. It was a life of waiting, nerve-racking waiting. Once in a while a displaced hope buried deep within brought tears to the eyes. As for now, still in the depths of a dark pit, the men remained shadows, wandering around the magic circle surrounded by wires and mines. Up at five, breakfast at six, back to the stalls, dinner at three, every other day half an hour outside, then sunset and the first signs of dusk.

All of Manjača was imbued with a heavy, melancholy aroma. Even the mountain could be counted among the conspirators. The dark night air was so thick it could be cut with a knife. The birds flew so high that the sound of their flapping wings was inaudible. With no mountain spring close by for rejuvenation and no thick shade to give shelter from the sun, there was nothing there that made a mountain a mountain, and people people.

Djemo was in Number Six. Futko and Ramiz, friends from the old neighborhood, were right next to him. Muharem and Sanel were across the way. They had a little over a foot between them to serve as a passageway. Futko and Ramiz worked in the kitchen and often managed to sneak some food out for Djemo. Djemo shared it with Muharem and Sanel. Mursel also worked in the kitchen. When they dished out the food, Mursel put out more than the single spoonful rationed to each prisoner. After the bread was sliced, he took the crumbs and put them in a bowl with gravy to share with his hungry companions.

During the last month the food got even better. For breakfast they were given a cup of milk or tea, a quarter of a loaf of bread, and a small can of fish. For lunch they also got a quarter of a loaf of bread with gravy, beans, lentils, and potatoes. On rare occasions there was even a piece of meat in the gravy.

The days followed one after another. They got shorter and shorter. By early afternoon the sun was already ducking behind the tallest mountain peak, right where a big Serbian flag was flying. The chill of the mountain air stole into the stalls. The dog days somehow managed to pass, but the nights seemed endless.

More often than not, Djemo played chess with Muharem with the board and pieces he and Nedžad had made. Šišić also played; he won some and lost some, and every now and then he got angry. Sometimes Djemo just sat by himself, alone with his thoughts. He stared off into the distance at some point over the roof, his pale face shrouded in sadness. With his right hand he straightened the dirty bandage on his left. Then he would pull the small photographs of his sons out of his pocket, the photos Alma had sent him while he was still in Omarska, and his face would become wet with tears.

A few days earlier he had gotten a message from his wife through the Red Cross. She wrote:

I know how it was for you in Omarska and on the road to Manjača. My dear Djemo, you just have to see it through for our sake, but most of all for your son Deni. I had never imagined how much he would miss you. He thinks and talks about you constantly. When he eats, he always puts a plate and silverware next to his place and says "This is for my dad." It isn't easy to go through all that with him every day, but this will all pass and be over someday, it has to. Deni reads your letter aloud and brings us all to tears. He wants me to tell you that on October 1, at exactly one o'clock—the time of his birth—you should take his picture and kiss it so that will be a way for you to wish him a Happy Birthday. And he'll kiss your picture. . . .

Today he told me: "Mama, take me to the Red Cross, so I can ask them to take me to see my father, and if they did take me to him, not even God could separate us." He doesn't eat well, and he's lost a lot of weight. He only eats when I tell him to do it for your sake. In his room today I found a letter that he wants to send to Banja Luka TV. It's written just like a grownup. Here, I'll give you a few sentences so you can see for yourself: "Anyone who can help me contact my dad and see that my dear dad returns to me, should please get in touch with me. I pledge you my very own young life that my dad has no connection to this crazy war, or to weapons and politics."

When they searched the house he was talking to them, explaining everything, his eyes full of tears and fear. We are leaving Prijedor soon. We have to. We can't stay here any longer. Every day they take someone else away and no one ever sees them again. I am afraid for Ari; he is already too grown up. We are leaving, and we don't know where we're going. You'll get in touch with us through your brother Tewfik. . . . Love from Alma, Deni, and Ari.

Djemo read the letter for the hundredth time, and once again he felt like a cannonball had lodged in his throat, suffocating him and making him want to cry out in pain. Through the Red Cross the prisoners received messages once a month. These were turned over to the camp administration and held for up for ten days, to be read and censored. Prisoners had to wait more than a month to get an answer to messages they had sent. Everyone gathered around and listened in rapt attention on letter day. If a prisoner's name was called, he broke out into a grin. Those who weren't called remained silent, waiting for the next time. Yesterday some names had been called. There were messages for Asaf and Dr. Eso Sadiković. "Eso, if you are still breathing somewhere under the sky, let us know. Your family is waiting for you." That's what his wife, Cica, wrote. This message, along with Asaf's, was returned. Their loved ones would have to search for them somewhere else maybe.

Djemo looked at the photos of Ari and Deni again, and his eyes misted over. He wiped his face with his dirty sleeve and began to read the message once more: "Exactly at one o'clock." Today was Deni's birthday, October 1. Today, exactly at one o'clock, in about half an hour, he would be eleven years old. And this was the first time his father wouldn't be there on his birthday. He couldn't hold back the tears any longer. Muharem came over and said, "I know how hard it is, my friend, but we're going to make it through somehow. Don't be ashamed, go ahead and cry, you'll feel better. It's for your son that you're crying. Look, I'm even crying. Your son is proud of you, of that you can be sure. He knows damn well you aren't guilty of anything." Muharem, his eyes full of tears as well, patted Djemo on the shoulder. The words seemed to slide from his dried-up lips.

At exactly one o'clock Djemo took the little picture and kissed it. Once again he felt that cannonball in his throat. He took a bit of the dried-up fern from the floor, crumbled it up, rolled it into a piece of old newspaper, and lit it. He chased away at the wisps of smoke for a long time and looked at the photograph, dwelling on memories of other times. A big cake on the table, candles, the toast of full glasses, and the smell of fresh roasted meat, all his friends together, music. . . . Thousands of unspoken desires reeled through his mind.

The day slipped by slowly. At sunset rosy light came through the cracks in the wooden fence of the stall and played about his face. Djemo felt like his companions were passing shadows counting the days and marking them off in the far reaches of their minds. They cut holes in their blankets and tossed them over their shoulders, like ponchos. Nowhere does night so stealthily weave men into its web as in the mountains. Long shadows instantly turn into an overwhelming black silence. The men huddled together in their stalls to stay warm, clutching to themselves the blankets with DEUTSCHE ROTES KREUTZ written across them. The wind stole through the cracks and made the flame on the single small oil lantern dance, almost extinguishing it. Shreds of plastic sheeting tacked under the roof flapped in the breeze. Only an occasional shadow moved between the rows, by the door.

A big tin drum cut in half had become the night toilet. The men would take care of their needs, emptying out their ailing guts right next to other prisoners sleeping only a few feet away. An unbearable stench filled the entire stall. Some prisoners crawled still further under their blankets, covering up their heads. Others fell asleep quickly, emitting strange sounds from their throats. Many just lay awake, waiting for sleep to overtake them.

Then the rain would begin. When it rained, dozens of field mice came in through the cracks in the wall, scratching at the cement bulge overhead, scurrying over their blankets and even crawling under them. When Futko found a mouse in his box of cookies, he just grabbed it to give Ramiz a scare. Right beneath his head under the blanket in the fern pile, Halil from Glamoč found a nest with four tiny newborn mice. Their eyes hadn't even opened yet, and they still didn't have any fur. It was only at Manjača that many of the prisoners came to realize that a mouse can crawl straight up a wall. The men got used to the presence of the mice and often left tiny bread crumbs out for them.

Many prisoners woke in the night from the cold; they paced back and forth in their stalls, wrapping their blankets tight around them as they rubbed their hands together to generate a little warmth before crawling back to their spot on the fern bedding. The shift on duty woke them up at five o'clock. The guards would open the doors, which had been bolted all night, and let out groups of ten men to go to the toilet. The toilet itself was nothing more than two strong planks about ten feet long laid across a trench dug into the ground; overhead, a few asbestos tiles were supposed to serve as something like a roof. During their stay at Manjača, every couple of weeks the prisoners dug a new trench and moved the whole contraption.

The shovels and picks used to dig these holes had to be returned to the administration building every night, just as the cooks had to turn in their kitchen knives.

Chapter Nine

A winding dirt road to the right of the kitchen led in the direction of Banja Luka. As the prisoners ate their rations, they would raise their eyes and look longingly in the direction of the road, as if they were expecting something. The road came to a dead end at the camp. Not far away, beside a curve in the road, a tall chimney emerged from the ground. Before anyone arrived at the camp, the prisoners could first see a cloud of dust near the chimney. Then they could make out the shape of cars or trucks as they dipped in and out of view, driving along the curves behind the hills. Soon the sounds of an engine could be heard. Usually it was the Red Cross or camp officials. When the supply trucks came, the cloud of dust was even bigger.

"When will our buses out of here raise some dust?" Raif Zukanović asked from the kitchen, wistfully glancing at the road and then sighing out loud. "We have a ways to go before we see that day," Muharem answered, waiting in line for his rations. "Don't bet on it, Muharem," Djemo said. "I don't think we'll be here long enough to see real winter come," and he seemed to sense an echo of approval and encouragement. "We'll see winter, don't you worry, *and* spring."

Then Eso, a man from Kozarac who was standing right behind Muharem, said, "I doubt it, we'll be long gone. Today I overheard the vet talking to the commander. He said all the cattle they put out of these stalls that are now grazing on the hills will die if they don't bring them back in under cover." "So that means those cows might save our lives?" Muharem chimed in again, smiling. "Someone has to. If people won't, then it might as well be cows," Djemo added.

"I heard some foreign journalists came," said Raif, changing the topic. "Now they're saying in the administration that they'll come again and take our pictures." That very day, in fact, the French minister of health, Bernard Couchener, along with a TV crew, had visited Manjača. The Frenchmen talked to a few prisoners and filmed some interviews under the constant surveillance of the camp's head officials, who registered every single word.

Osme Didović, from Gornja Sanica, had his picture taken more than any other prisoner. Osme, a real living corpse, weighed only about sixty-five pounds. He had been arrested at home and taken to the police station in Ključ. Two days later they transferred him to the school auditorium in Sitnica, about twenty miles from Ključ. From there, Osme and about four hundred other residents of Gornja Sanica were taken on foot to Manjača.

It took only about ten minutes for the reporters to be told that their time with the prisoners was up; the officials led them out of the pavilion toward the gate. Later a lot of other crews came and told the prisoners that the world knew about them now, that pictures from Manjača had circled the globe. Some of the television crews brought cigarettes, handing them out to the prisoners one at a time. The journalists often had to fight back their own tears. TV crews from RTL, the BBC, and CNN and journalists from all the largest magazines and papers around the world, they all came.

The Red Cross representatives continued to come every Wednesday. They told us that talks were being held among the three parties in Bosnia regarding the closing of the camps; progress was very slow, but they were hopeful it wouldn't drag on too much longer. The prisoners were also told that they wouldn't be going home after their release but would be sent to a third country willing to take them in and give them asylum until the political situation in Bosnia-Herzegovina was resolved. "A number of countries have already volunteered to take you in: Germany, Holland, America, Norway, New Zealand, and many others." "You offer us half the world, but all we want is our Bosnia," whispered Djemo, the words trembling in his throat. He felt a tear rolling down his cheek. He wasn't sure whether it was from the smoke of Muharem's cigarette or his acute feeling of helplessness. Again Muharem noticed and added, "How I wish I could just start singing 'Don't

Give up, Bosnia,' at the top of my lungs." But the words caught in his throat, and he winced and gripped his rib cage under his blanket cape.

Later Djemo got a message from his brother Tewfik, saying that his wife and sons had gotten onto a convoy traveling from Prijedor to Zagreb via Vlašić, Travnik, and Split. Halid Muslimović had picked them up in Zagreb and taken them to his place in Klagenfurt, Austria. Halid was Djemo's best friend. Foreseeing what was to come, he had left Prijedor with his family long before and had tried to convince Djemo to follow along. Knowing his family was safe and far away from all the horror made it much easier for Djemo to go on.

"In Bosnia, even the sun is drenched in blood," Muharem used to say. "Even the sun has been caught up in these wholesale death sentences." Little by little they lost all sense of time, the one thing they had more than enough of to spare. As the present ebbed away, the lack of any purpose except survival was slowly destroying them. They were only numbers, shadows: heads down, hands behind their backs. A trace of vulnerability crept into their fragile bodies.

Every prisoner under forty was taken out daily for

forced labor. After breakfast they were lined up in front of the gate and sent off to work in groups, with an armed escort. Some took care of the livestock, dug up potatoes in the nearby fields, or shucked corn by the gate. Others went into the forest by truck, five or six miles from camp, to cut and load firewood. The soldiers then drove the trucks full of firewood to their own houses or sold it, taking the proceeds as pay for their "loyalty" to the Serbian army. Rumor had it that in the merciless woodcutting, many prisoners were "cut down" as well. A prisoner from Kozarac used to drive the truck used for firewood. The truck itself had once been his own, before it was confiscated during the attacks on Kozarac.

Enis and Fiko worked in the garage, right next to the administration building. Occasionally, when the guard was far enough away, they managed to turn on the radio of the car they were working on and listen to the news so they could spread the word later among the prisoners. Sometimes the shuckers tossed a ripe ear of corn across the wire when the guard wasn't looking. These would be cooked over the fire in the kitchen or sold for a cigarette or two.

A guard by the name of Stojšić once caught a prisoner throwing an ear of corn over and gave him a hell of a beating in front of everyone. Stojšić hit him with both hands at the same time, his palms open, a technique that happened to be his specialty. Afterward Stojšić went into Number Six, the first stall next to the gates, and made everyone do pushups. He howled as they vainly tried to lift their emaciated bodies. Another time a guard on watch whose name was Predojević went into Number Six to look for a prisoner he heard had sold his blanket for cigarettes. When no one gave himself up, Predojević ordered twenty of the men from the first row, including Djemo, and another twenty from the second row to stand quietly without moving for three full hours. The prisoners began calling him "Ali Baba": Djemo and the rest of them were the forty thieves.

A soldier from Banja Luka named Zoka once beat two older prisoners just because they stepped out in front of the stall without asking for permission. He hit them in the stomach with his knee at least ten times in a row, one after the other. Špaga, the supervisor, happened to come along, and in front of everyone he said:

"What the hell do you think you're doing? Why are you beating these men? Either one of them could be your father. Pack your stuff and haul your ass off to Banja Luka this minute." Everyone knew very well what that meant. Zoka would be sent to the front at Derventa or Gradačac. Two days later word came that Zoka had committed suicide. In his own home in Banja Luka, he had put a pistol to his mouth and pulled the trigger.

That wasn't the first time Špaga had stood up for the prisoners. He used to cruise around the camp on a Vespa, sometimes even pulling into the stalls. Sitting on the scooter, he'd look up at the roof with a smile and comment, "How nice, I see you've already decorated the place," pointing to the cobwebs that had gathered between the rafters. "All you need now is Santa Claus, and you'll be all set for New Year's." "Didn't I tell you we'd be here for the winter," Muharem said, adding a refrain to his pessimistic forecast.

"No way, Muharem," responded Miro Turnušek, who used to be the director of a large baked goods factory in Prijedor. "There's no way we'll survive a winter here in these conditions. When there's ten feet of snow in these craggy mountains, you can't even bring supplies in. Even if they had a warehouse full of food, we'd all freeze to death."

"Then what are all those stoves doing out there?" Muharem asked, referring to the stoves the Red Cross had brought in a few days earlier, at the request of the camp administration. "Come on, Muharem, you know just as well as me that not even the furnaces in the steel mills at Zenica could heat these stalls up, much less those dinky little things," Djemo said. "Of course, I know that, so why'd they bring them here?" Then Miro, even though he knew it wouldn't be easy to crack Muharem's bleak perspective, stepped in and said: "Look, they also hauled in all that plumbing out there, but that still doesn't mean we've got any water; they get all the diesel they want, but that still doesn't mean we're going to stop going to the lake with our bottles. It's all a game. They're just playing for more time."

Then someone behind them joined in: "I heard there's going to be a call-up today. Some of the guys are going in an exchange." Someone else, a reporter from Radio Sarajevo, Feho Sarhatlić, sat down next to them and lit up a cigarette: "I heard it from Šemso, our guy on duty, who said he overheard Špaga talking it over with a soldier." That afternoon twenty-four men were called. Among them was Feho himself. He packed up his few things and sadly shook his head. Taking a long look at a photo of his five-year-old son, he brushed his brow with the edge of his sleeve, put the picture back in with his things, and went out to the gate. Half an hour later a khaki-colored army bus drove past the mess; it continued to raise dust as it meandered along the winding dirt road toward the chimney before fading out of sight.

Early the next morning, even before breakfast, all the Croats were called up. They were told to get their things ready in fifteen minutes and line up in front of the gate. As they were loaded into four buses, the prisoners made sure to take their water bottles, having learned from the experience of the trip from Omarska to Manjača that it was impossible to know how long such a trip could take. This time the escorts were new, soldiers from Banja Luka. As soon as the buses got going, one of the soldiers went from prisoner to prisoner, giving each a handful of salt with an order to eat it. "If I find even one grain of salt in your hand or under your seat, you'll remember me real well," he threatened, slapping his truncheon into the open palm of his left hand and smiling brazenly.

Among the prisoners was a man named Nono; he was the director of Hotel Prijedor, someone everybody knew and got along well with. Nono brought the salt to his mouth and touched it with his tongue, but the taste made him want to throw up immediately. Rather than take such a risk, he waited until the soldier had turned his attention to something else and then poured the salt into his sock, being very careful not to spill any on the floor. He left just a little in his hand and continued to lick it as his face twisted in a grimace.

The soldier strolled among the seats with a sneer, slamming a prisoner with his truncheon every now and then as the bus continued through Ključ and Bosanski Petrovac to Drvar. At Drvar two more soldiers got in and began hitting the prisoners with blackjacks right away. One hoisted himself up on the luggage racks on either side of the aisle and kicked his way down the ribs and stomachs of the prisoners the whole length of the bus. "I know you want to get out of here in good shape, so the face and head is off limits. I'll just knock out your kidneys!" The crazed soldier laughed maniacally as he continued kicking them.

In the afternoon they reached Knin, a town about thirty miles from the coast that had become known as the capital of the Serbian Republic of Krajina. "In about half an hour, along with representatives from UNPROFOR, we will reach the border dividing us from the Croatian forces. There you will be exchanged for Serbs who were prisoners in their camps. When we arrive, get off the bus two at a time and move toward their buses. Don't try anything stupid, because you'll pay with your life. This is war," said one of the Serbian officials, adorned with insignias on his cap and the sleeves of his uniform. Apparently, he was supposed to be some kind of Serb minister. The bus kept going past Knin, stopping about five miles beyond Drniš. The prisoners stayed in their seats with their heads down and waited. They waited like that an hour or two, maybe more. "Take them back to Knin," said the minister, standing in front of the buses. "The exchange didn't come off, we'll try again tomorrow."

They were taken back to Knin and put into a cell

block in the prison of a military barracks. The escorting soldiers went off to sleep, and the responsibility for guarding the prisoners was taken over by the locals, members of the special "Knin Boys," notorious for their exploits. All trained in the martial arts, they were almost always ready to show off their prowess. Kicks and long blackjacks were their methods of choice; they also liked inviting their civilian friends to join in the fun, railing at Tudjman and Croatia, cursing the prisoners' *Ustasha* mothers. This went on until well after midnight. Finally they tired themselves out and took a breather.

In the morning the prisoners were led outside into a fenced-off area and ordered to sing *chetnik* songs. About noon the escorts arrived only to say that the exchange was not going to happen, that even the Croats' own people didn't want them, and they were loaded back onto the buses they had come on for the return trip.

"Anyone know how to sing?" a soldier asked, as they made their way toward Bosansko Grahovo and Drvar. "I do," volunteered someone from the back of the bus. "Who's that? Come on, speak up, let's have a look at you." It was Milutin Dimač, a young man who used to sing in cafés all over Bosnia. Even though he wasn't exactly in the mood to sing, he figured his singing might at least save some of his friends from a worse beating. "Up front, come on up here," the soldier said, sending a prisoner sitting in the front seat back to take Milutin's place. "You know the song 'The Soldiers Danced in the Middle of the Land of Serbia?'" "Sure," answered Milutin, as he began to sing with a bit of a tremor, even though he held the melody well. He sang all the rest of the way back to Manjača, taking an occasional break for a cigarette or a sip of plum brandy offered by the soldiers. "You sing those songs good, just like a Serb," one of the soldiers snickered. They got to Manjača around nine in the evening, and only then did they get something to eat.

Later word spread that a Croatian officer who was at Manjača and had been put on the list wasn't taken along by the Serbs with the other prisoners; when the Croats realized this, they called off the exchange. The next day Feho Sarhatlić and his group came back from another exchange that had fallen through. They had been taken to Mount Vlašić, overlooking Travnik. They hadn't been beaten and were even fed. A few days later Feho, Nono, Edin Škulja (a painter from Glamoč), and another eight men were called up. The other prisoners soon found out that they went across at Vlašić and that finally a successful exchange had been completed.

But large clouds continued to drift over Manjača, that gathering place of sorrow. Clouds of dust on the dirt road marked each arrival, stirring the smoldering embers of hope. "Good God!" Djemo said, raising his hands toward the sky, as if he were addressing someone. "Look at everyone, look them straight in the eye, look into their faces, look at their wasted bodies," and again he felt the inaudible noise of tears trickling down his cheek. Would anyone understand the tragedy of these men, linked by fate to this place? Sorrow had darkened their visages and twisted their faces. Their hair had turned white from fear. They cried out in their sleep, reliving scenes of horror. All the prisoners desperately wanted to forget all the horror, but the angel of death's carelessness had marked them as witnesses. When would some light begin to penetrate the obscurity? Djemo's eyes expressed only doubt. He looked across the wavy hills surrounding them and the wide plateau in front of the camp. The sound of distant explosions reached his ears.

"It's going to rain again, hear the thunder?" he said.

"They're shelling Jajce," Muharem interrupted. "Today they took some of our men down to the barracks. They ordered them to load mortar shells onto trucks. They say there are hangars full of them."

"He who lives by the sword, dies by the sword," someone added. As night fell, so did the rain.

That night barking dogs broke the silence of the camp as occasional rounds fired off in the distance could be heard. In the morning they learned that some prisoners had escaped and a search team was out looking for them. The soldiers on duty were in a foul mood and didn't let a single prisoner leave the stall that day.

"It was that shepherd, Halil's son, and his friend that was always with him," Muharem, informed as always, told Djemo. "They took off last night around seven, during the fog. Imagine, they went across the minefield after they'd marked all the detonators sticking out of the ground with empty sardine cans. They jumped the barbed wire, snitched two of the best horses from the stall next door, saddled them up, and took off into the night. Later the guards organized a posse, that's why we heard the shots and the barking. But they didn't catch them, because they got a good head start, and besides, Halil's son knows every nook and cranny around here because this is where he used to graze his sheep. They took all the food they'd been buying from the cook for cigarettes and storing up. And they each had three blankets."

Later Halil, the old shepherd, was called in by the officials. They asked whether he knew that his son had intended to escape and what route he might have taken. Halil insisted that he knew nothing, that he hadn't even talked with his son recently, and that he had no idea where they might have gone. Halil was not beaten, only told that, if he learned anything, he should report it to them through the guards and soldiers on duty. Much later Halil learned that the two escapees had reached Livno, where they enlisted to join the forces defending Bosnia-Herzegovina. "For the last month or so, before the escape, I really didn't speak to my son. We even had a big argument in front of all the prisoners. But we worked all that out between ourselves beforehand, so I wouldn't spoil his escape," Halil said later.

Theirs was the only successful escape from Man-jača. Earlier, two men from Kozarac, Šahbaz and Bešić, ran off into the forest where they had been on a fire-wood detail with about twenty other prisoners. When they went further into the woods for a new load, they just didn't stop. It took about five or six hours for any-one to notice they were missing. The soldiers organized a manhunt for them. Šahbaz and Bešić didn't know Manjača very well, but they knew roughly what direc-tion they should head in. If they went west, they'd even-tually get closer to Prijedor, and that was home turf. They spent the night on the straw in a barn, just at the edge of a Serbian village. They didn't even stay the whole night, just two or three hours to rest a little and make sure the soldiers weren't on their trail. They set out again way before the break of dawn, through woods and empty spaces. About noon the next day they got to Sanski Most. No one noticed them as they blended in with the crowd before getting on a bus headed for Prije-dor. There they even managed to have a beer at a little café. And then they went further, on foot, through long forgotten paths, toward Kozarac.

For a few nights they slept in the ruins of Kozarac

before heading toward Mount Kozara and the Sava River, with the idea of getting to free territory in Croatia. They got only as far as Bosanska Orahova, a Muslim village on the right bank of the Sava. Šahbaz had an aunt there, and they spent the night at her place. Most of the residents of Orahova were still in their homes, since they had turned their weapons over without a fight and the Serbs hadn't begun harassing them yet.

Early in the morning Šahbaz and Bešić set out to cross the Sava. Šahbaz swam across first. He forded the wide river easily, and no one saw him. Bešić wasn't much of a swimmer and couldn't bring himself to take the plunge. Šahbaz waved at him from the other side, but Bešić just waded out a ways before heading back to shore. Šahbaz finally swam back, since he didn't want to abandon his friend.

Afterward a Serb patrol found them, and they were brought back to the Manjača camp in a military personnel carrier. They were beaten for days. One night after sunset, when all the prisoners were in their places, Šahbaz and Bešić were led from stall to stall as they were kicked and clubbed. The guards smashed their heads against the doors of the stall as they writhed with pain and screamed. But the two men managed to recover.

Another prisoner escaped from the potato patch, which was closer to camp. No one ever heard what happened to him. If the Serbs caught him, he certainly wasn't brought back to Manjača.

Chapter Ten

The sun cooled off above the mountain as the days got shorter. Rain clouds hovered over the camp, unloading their burden to turn into muddy, limestone-laden puddles. The puddles held the prints of the soaked shoes of the drained prisoners, who started to resemble the earth themselves. Their paltry bodies seemed to be covered in a yellowish film, as if they had been dipped in wax. Their eyes, protruding from their sunken cheeks, reflected only sorrow.

As the days went by, their hopes, too, sank further

behind the mountains. Fewer and fewer prayers were offered to the sky above. Their gazes stayed more and more on the ground as their backs bent. Some slept with their eyes open, staring at the cracks in the roof overhead as the snow gradually drifted in. The reflection of the flame from the glass lantern played on the faces of those closest to the door. They pulled their caps on tight over their closely shaven heads. Apples were given out, but the fruit stuck in their throats. Their unending powerlessness overtook the prisoners, and the days fell away like beads off a broken string of prayer beads in the hands of a nonbeliever. More and more often the snow lent a silver coating to the plateau; up higher in the mountains, the roofs were covered. A thick, unsavory fog hung in the space between the stalls.

"Didn't I tell you we'd be here all winter," Muharem commented, as whirling snow twisted outside and the wind howled sadly through the cracks in the walls.

"You don't even know what winter in Manjača means," replied his neighbor, Alija, blowing on his numbed hands. "This is just the first sign, but don't go asking for trouble, we've got enough as it is."

Harač, a truly generous and kind man from the next stall, joined in. "Last night I dreamed that I made it home, but it wasn't a good dream. When I got home, no one was there."

"Last night I saw a falling star, and it left a long shimmering trail," said Baim, a police inspector from Sanski Most. "It took me a long time to fall asleep after that. While I was thinking things over, I remembered some lines of poetry. I came up with a whole poem about us and our tribulations, but I had already forgotten it by morning. I only remember one of the lines that I used at the beginning: 'Such times finally came, I am here just because of my name.'"

"Everything is right in line with the Geneva accords," added Muharem.

"While you were composing that poem," Harač said, looking at Baim, "I was being beaten in the administration building."

Everyone's attention turned to Harač. "They called me last night, just after sunset, and took me to the administration building, into an office. There was only one soldier with me. Afterward another one came in and asked how come I was there. I thought I recognized the voice, and I raised my head to see the face of my oldest son, Denis. I stood quietly for a while, just confused, and then I asked, 'Whose army are you in anyway, son?' Denis didn't say anything. I looked at him like that for a long time, trying to catch his eye, but he stood there perplexed, with his head turned to one side. 'Fuck that army of yours, son,' I told him, and I couldn't help saying it to him even though I was crying. Denis left, without answering me. Then the other soldier beat me, and there was crying and screaming from the office next door." Harač finished up his story, hardly able to contain himself as he recounted this new emotional twist: "I never want to see him again so long as he's wearing the uniform of those scumbags. I don't care if he's my son a hundred times over."

A hush fell over everyone. No one wanted to set off the charged feelings coursing through the air after Harač's confession. After a minute or two, a huge explosion ripped through the sky. Gravel, crushed stone, and clumps of soil came raining down on the other side of the stall next to them. The word traveled fast: a prisoner from Kotor Varoš accidentally stepped on a mine and lost both his legs while he was stretching his freshly washed shirt out to dry on the barbed wire. One of his legs from the knee down, together with the shoe, had fallen on the roof of the neighboring stall.

In a panic, the soldiers drove all the prisoners into the stall and ordered them to close the doors. Those closest to the doors saw the poor guy being carried off toward the administration building by Dr. Mensur and two soldiers. The man's other leg, crushed and bloody, hung by pieces of skin. He was taken by car to the hospital in Banja Luka but died there in a couple of days. He had lost too much blood for his depleted body to recover from the injury.

Five other prisoners ended up at the same hospital after eating mushrooms that turned out to be poisonous when they were working in the forest.

With the first days of November, a few changes took place. The International Red Cross representatives began to visit the prisoners nearly every day, assuring them that Manjača would be closing very soon. The pied pipers also began to act differently toward the prisoners. They let the prisoners out of their stalls whenever they liked and the weather permitted, at least during the day. The prisoners would walk around on the tiled area between the stalls, until sunset, and then withdraw to their own stalls. And so it went, day after day. The only break in this monotonous routine was the shattering sound of Serb planes as they careened just above the roofs of the barn. The prisoners who knew something about planes said they were breaking the sonic barrier, right there above them at Manjača. The guards raised their heads at the deafening clap and looked high up into the sky, smiling over the roar until the planes disappeared behind the peaks, leaving a thin, misty trail behind them.

Twice a week representatives from Merhamet, a Muslim humanitarian organization in Banja Luka, delivered packages of food and clothing that had been sent by the prisoners' relatives. According to camp regulations, only fifty packages at a time could be brought in. The packages were first given to the guards on duty, who carefully picked through them. Cigarettes, fruit, chocolate, and better clothing were set aside and divided up among the guards; only then were the prisoners called to be given what was left of their packages. All the letters were examined and usually thrown out. Only rarely did a prisoner's face brighten as a message actually got into his hands.

Every day there was more and more talk about the camp breaking up. Rumor had it that Karadžić himself had signed an agreement to that effect. The prisoners waited impatiently from early morning every day the Red Cross was due.

Friday, November 13, was a foggy morning with snow in the air. Like so many of the preceding days, the prisoners had more time to kill than they could possibly know what to do with. Around noon all of them were ordered back into their stalls. Most figured they were being set up for yet another visit by reporters who would be eager to talk and take pictures of their emaciated bodies. But right before lunch a soldier came into the stall and said, "Everybody whose name I call, run out and line up in front of the gate, double time."

"Should they take their stuff or not?" someone asked.

"No, leave everything," the soldier answered, adding that everyone born in 1950 or before, and everyone born in 1972 or after, should get ready. He held a long list and read out the last names of the prisoners in alphabetical order.

"Probably another exchange," Muharem said. "But even if it doesn't go through, it's better than just staying here without knowing what's going to happen next. When were you born?"

"1949. I'm in," answered Djemo.

"Good. At least we'll be together, whatever happens, who knows . . . ," and then Muharem almost seemed to glow as something like a smile fought its way across his face.

Djemo was among the first to be called. He went out and joined the small group of prisoners the soldiers had lined up in front of the gate. Their names were called out again as they were divided into groups of fifty, five to a line. Each prisoner was told to remember his exact spot within his group. An officer came to address them: "Tomorrow you will be leaving the Manjača camp. As of tomorrow, representatives of the International Red Cross will assume responsibility over you. You will be transferred to the transit center in Karlovac, and from there you will be moved to a third country, where you will remain until this war is over. Tomorrow, before you leave, you will have to sign a written consent agreeing to this. The order of the groups in which you are now standing is the same order in which you will board your buses. Now go back to your pavilions."

Even this voice had a pleasant ring to the prisoners' ears. It was as if the black birds auguring ill fate had suddenly taken off and left them alone. Finally someone had pronounced the words they had been waiting to hear for months. All the accumulated hope they had kept in check started to function again. A hesitant mixture of joy and confusion spread across their faces, as if they had just ascended from the deepest circle of hell. Djemo felt a sweet tremor work its way through his body from head to toe. Muharem couldn't wipe the smile off his face.

Back in the stall, Šukrija Topalović, a famous soccer referee who used to play cards with Djemo all the time, hugged Djemo and Muharem and through his tears said: "My friends, as sorry as I am that I'm staying, I can't even begin to tell you how happy I am that you're leaving. Maybe we'll also be going soon. At least things are finally moving." Muharem was crying: "I still can't believe all of this is actually happening. My heart feels like it's going to jump out of my skin!"

That night they couldn't sleep. Ramiz and Futko brought a lot of food and fruit from the kitchen and distributed it to those preparing for the trip. They weren't among the lucky ones, at least this time around. The men sang together quietly, until it got very late. In the morning, right after breakfast, those who were leaving packed up their things. Djemo said good-bye to all the men he had gotten to know. It was hardest for him to part with Futko. Djemo didn't say a word, but his trembling body and tears expressed more than anything he could have said.

Djemo turned around and headed for the gate, where everybody was already lining up according to plan. When they were all in order, the commander of the camp, Lieutenant Colonel Božidar Popović, addressed them: "I hope we meet again, but over coffee or a drink. I wouldn't like to see you here again. Make sure you don't get brought back to this camp or any other camps, because next time around you might not be so lucky. Now you're off to some other country, but I know you'll come back someday, back home, when this crazy war is over. War is worthless, but it can't last forever. I wish you all the best."

Špaga, the supervisor, called out the names of the prisoners again one by one; as they were called, they went through the gate of the camp and boarded the buses lined up outside. Djemo was in Number Six, and Muharem was in the fourth bus behind him. Altogether there were fourteen buses, with about seven hundred prisoners—that is, men who were about to become ex-prisoners.

Djemo nervously tried to pull himself together in his seat, still not believing that this bus was taking him straight to freedom. Everyone got a pack of cigarettes and a bag of food and fruit for the trip, in addition to what Futko and Ramiz had pilfered from the kitchen. Brand-new blankets were folded and already waiting on the seats for some of the weaker men. The haste and diligence of the International Red Cross workers won the open and heartfelt appreciation of the men on the buses, as well as those left behind the barbed-wire fence of the camp, tearfully waving good-bye to their friends and relatives.

Only one soldier, sitting to the right of the driver, served as an escort on Djemo's bus. He didn't even look twenty. He spread himself out comfortably with his rifle leaning next to him; when the bus started off, he told Djemo and the others: "Just a little longer, and you'll all be free. As far as I'm concerned, you're already free. Relax, talk, have a smoke. You just can't get off the bus until we get to Novska." When the bus drove by the canteen, Djemo saw Futko, Ramiz, and a few other prisoners waving at them from the kitchen. "Two of my sons are still there," said an older man sitting behind Djemo. "I asked if they'd let them out and keep me instead, but they wouldn't." As he let out a deep sigh, Djemo turned to look at the camp and everyone in it one last time.

They drove along the same dirt road they had come in on from Omarska, through the forest and the woods, going down the mountainside toward the main road, which went on toward Banja Luka. The column of buses was led by a vehicle from the International Red Cross, its big red flag flying high. Before getting onto the main road, the buses were stopped by a military checkpoint at the intersection. Djemo's bus stopped right next to a house with people milling around who didn't seem the least bit happy about seeing such passengers. "It's a funeral for a Serb soldier," said the escort. "People are dying like flies. Who needed this war in the first place?" He just kept on talking, while the prisoners could hardly wait for the bus to get going again. It finally took off; before they knew it, they were going past Banja Luka on the side road. The streets were filled with people. The cowering faces of some and the uniforms of others made it very clear who was in control in the city.

The escort got off in Bosanska Gradiška, right before the bridge over the Sava River. At the crossing the buses were joined by UNPROFOR's armed soldiers wearing blue helmets and the insignia of the UN. After driving twenty miles through ravaged Croatian villages, they reached Novska. Once there, the column turned into a huge parking lot next to the highway. About fifty yards away the men could see another column of buses parked alongside the road. They were led out in groups, now escorted by the Red Cross, and taken to these other buses. "Now you really are free," the men were told, as their escorts rejoiced in the happiness of their new charges. "I just feel like hugging these people, even though I've never seen them before in my life," someone said.

Finally they had crossed that invisible line marking a return to life. They sobbed and cried from happiness. The men embraced, as if they hadn't seen each other in ages, and the joy radiated through their bodies, illuminating their faces. Rivers of blessed tears drowned out all traces of sorrow. Djemo felt like his heart would leap out of his chest as he shivered in delight.

He took his things and hopped onto one of the buses. Droves of reporters and TV crews milled around. From the radio in the bus Djemo heard the news: "Today the Serb authorities have freed 740 prisoners from the notorious camp at Manjača." Djemo went back outside. "Djemo, are we dreaming all this?" Muharem asked, stretching his arms up high over his head. "I just feel like screaming at the top of my lungs, so they could hear me over on the other side of the Sava and the Una, and even further!"

Djemo sobbed. Then he turned to face Mount Kozara, and his eyes wandered off into the distance, his expression changing into one of deep longing. "My Prijedor is over there," he whispered. "I don't know if anyone could love that place more than I do. I'll be back, I promise. From now on, you're my battle cry!" He took a deep breath, wiped the tears from his cheek, raised his head, and clutching his hands in supplication, cried out: "Lord, may you never forgive them!"

And what next?

Those who've wounded the night—had already murdered the day.

Will they at least know how to feign repentance?

What will happen when they come to, when they wake up from this high-caliber dream?

What kind of visions will they weave then?

Will all the children they tortured and killed and crippled begin to speak through their children?

When the tainted iron is taken away from them, will that sediment of groundless hatred finally be sifted out of their consciousness?

Will they at least know how to mourn their own dead as they bury them armed in full regalia?

Will they at least, standing at their own graves, teach their children not to grow up seeking revenge?

Will the sense of justice everyone is born with still prevail within them as well?

I am only one of many whose eyes beheld unrelent-

ing misery every day, whose entrails faced their incandescent barrels, whose skin was flayed by their truncheons.

I am only one of many who still carries this heaviest of burdens wedged into the furthest reaches of my heart, these horrid scars, hoping that, in time, they will be rooted out and fade.